At Issue

School Shootings

Other books in the At Issue series:

Antidepressants
Are American Elections Fair?
Are Privacy Rights Being Violated?
Biological and Chemical Weapons
Child Labor and Sweatshops
Child Sexual Abuse
Creationism Versus Evolution
Does Advertising Promote Substance Abuse?
Does the World Hate the United States?
Do Infectious Diseases Pose a Serious Threat?
Do Nuclear Weapons Pose a Serious Threat?
Drug Testing
The Ethics of Capital Punishment
The Ethics of Euthanasia
The Ethics of Genetic Engineering
The Ethics of Human Cloning
Gay and Lesbian Families
Gay Marriage
Gene Therapy
How Can Domestic Violence Be Prevented?
How Does Religion Influence Politics?
How Should the World Respond to Natural Disasters?
Hurricane Katrina
Is the Mafia Still a Force in America?
Is Poverty a Serious Threat?
Legalizing Drugs
Prescription Drugs
Responding to the AIDS Epidemic
Steroids
What Causes Addiction?

At Issue

School Shootings

Susan Hunnicutt, Book Editor

GREENHAVEN PRESS

An imprint of Thomson Gale, a part of The Thomson Corporation

THOMSON

GALE

Detroit • New York • San Francisco • San Diego • New Haven, Conn.
Waterville, Maine • London • Munich

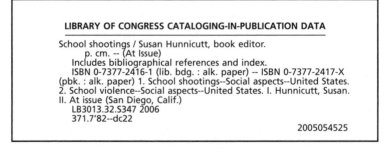

LIBRARY OF CONGRESS CATALOGING-IN-PUBLICATION DATA

School shootings / Susan Hunnicutt, book editor.
    p. cm. -- (At Issue)
  Includes bibliographical references and index.
    ISBN 0-7377-2416-1 (lib. bdg. : alk. paper) -- ISBN 0-7377-2417-X
(pbk. : alk. paper) 1. School shootings--Social aspects--United States.
2. School violence--Social aspects--United States. I. Hunnicutt, Susan.
II. At issue (San Diego, Calif.)
  LB3013.32.S347 2006
  371.7'82--dc22
                                                    2005054525

Printed in the United States of America
10 9 8 7 6 5 4 3 2 1

Contents

Introduction   7

1. School Shootings Are a Serious Problem   10
   Katherine S. Newman

2. The Media Exaggerate the School-   18
   Shooting Problem
   Joel Best

3. Violent Video Games Train School   28
   Shooters
   Jack Thompson

4. Violent Video Games Do Not Create   32
   School Shooters
   Henry Jenkins

5. Protecting Athletes Who Bully Other   39
   Students Promotes School Shootings
   Gary K. Clabaugh and Alison A. Clabaugh

6. Antidepressants May Trigger   46
   School Shootings
   Kelly Patricia O'Meara

7. Teaching Boys to Solve Problems with   55
   Violence Promotes School Shootings
   Seth Hicks

8. Overreacting to School Shootings   59
   Intensifies the Problem
   James Alan Fox and Jack Levin

9. Arming Teachers and Parents Will   63
   Prevent School Shootings
   Doug Hagin

10. Designing Safer Guns Will Reduce   **68**
    School Shootings

    Ronald Brownstein

11. Gun Control Laws Will Not Stop   **72**
    School Shootings

    Steve Chapman

12. School Testing Programs Overshadow   **76**
    School Shooting Prevention Programs

    Margaret McKenna and David Haselkorn

13. Victims of School Shootings Struggle to   **82**
    Rebuild Their Lives

    Vickie Bane and Jason Bane

Organizations to Contact   **90**

Bibliography   **95**

Index   **99**

Introduction

Two months after the April 1999 school shooting at Columbine High School in Littleton, Colorado, which took fifteen lives, Peggy Noonan, writing for *Good Housekeeping*, offered an evocative image: "What walked into Columbine High School . . . that day was the culture of death. This time it wore black trench coats. Last time [in Jonesboro, Arkansas,] it was children's hunting gear. Next time it will be some other costume, but it will still be the culture of death. . . . This is the ocean in which our children swim."

After such shootings commentators from across the political spectrum speculate about what would cause youths to open fire on their classmates and teachers. Many experts argue that popular culture, including television, movies, and music, are to blame.

One medium that receives intense scrutiny is the sniper video game. Virtually all school shooters have had prolonged engagement with "first person shooter" video games such as *DOOM* and *Mortal Kombat*, which strive for graphic and tactile realism in their virtual representations of gun violence. Some experts believe that violent video games train potential school shooters to kill. In consequence, they think that the government should tightly regulate their marketing. Others argue that violent video games are not a primary factor in school shootings and are protected from government control by the First Amendment. The issues explored in the debate over the role of violent video games are representative of other debates in the school shooting controversy.

In the opinion of some commentators, sniper video games are a primary factor in school shootings. Lt. Col. Dave Grossman, a West Point psychology professor, claims that video game makers are repackaging military training materials and marketing them to children who, through play, are becoming desensitized to the act of killing. In his 1999 book *Stop Teaching Our Kids to Kill,* Grossman recounts the story of the school shooting that took place in Paducah, Kentucky, in 1997. "Prior to stealing the gun, [Michael Carneal] had never shot a real handgun in his life.... So how many hits did Michael Carneal make? He fired eight shots; he got eight hits, on eight different kids. Five of them were head shots, and the other three were upper torso [shots]." Grossman says that Carneal's level of skill was extraordinary even by law enforcement standards and that he developed it by training on military-style killing simulators, "point and shoot video games he had played for hundreds of hours in video arcades and in the comfort of his own home." Grossman believes that to protect children and reduce the likelihood of school shootings, the marketing of sniper video games should be regulated. In testimony before the New York State Legislature, Grossman argues:

> It is the opinion of major experts in this area ... that violent video games are harmful to children. Legislation to rate these games, and enforcement of the ratings in order to keep the violent games out of the hands of children, is essential.... The games that permit a child to hold and aim a gun, and fire it at humans, are particularly harmful, since these devices teach shooting skills. They are firearms training devices at best, and murder simulators at worst.

Henry Jenkins, a professor of media studies at the Massachusetts Institute of Technology, acknowledges that all of the school shooters have also been game players. However, he disputes the claim that video games turned these young men into killers. "Ninety percent of boys and 40 percent of girls play [video games]. The overwhelming majority of kids who play do not commit antisocial acts," Jenkins maintains. He also argues that the military uses killing simulators as part of "a specific curriculum, with clearly defined goals, in a context where students actively want to learn and have a need for the information being transmitted." First person shooter games that are played in homes or arcades lack this overarching educational context, he contends. "Grossman's model only works," Jenkins asserts, "if we assume that [video game players] unwittingly apply what they learn in a fantasy environment to real world spaces." Douglas Lowenstein, president of the Interactive Digital Software Association agrees, adding that the First Amendment protects the content of sniper video games. "There is no compelling research which supports the belief that playing violent video games in the real world causes aggressive behavior in the real world.... Video games and computer games," he writes, "are protected forms of expression under our Constitution. Some may not like particular games, but the case law is clear that efforts by government to regulate violent content is unconstitutional."

While virtually all school shooters have played sniper video games, the relationship between these games and school shootings remains controversial. Since the First Amendment protects media expression, few agree on how best to protect children from any harmful effects these games might have. In an effort to understand the roots of school shootings and search for an appropriate response, the authors in *At Issue: School Shootings* debate these and other issues.

1

School Shootings Are a Serious Problem

Katherine S. Newman

Katherine S. Newman, sociology professor at the Woodrow Wilson School of Public and International Affairs at Princeton University, is author of Rampage: The Social Roots of School Shootings, *which is based on hours of interviews with witness-survivors of school shootings in Paducah, Kentucky, and Jonesboro, Arkansas.*

The second half of the 1990s and the beginning of the new century saw a measurable increase in the incidence of rampage school shootings that generated intense media coverage and public fear. Rampage shootings are different from other forms of school violence. For example, they take place on school campuses before an "audience" of fellow students, they involve multiple victims who are often chosen at random, and they are carried out by students or former students of the schools where they occur. The seemingly senseless loss of life in rampage school shootings creates intense fear nationwide, making rampage school shootings a serious problem that needs to be better understood.

The 1997–1998 academic year left a bloody trail of multiple-victim homicides in communities that imagined themselves violence free. Rampage school shootings had actu-

from the projects. . . . That's the city school. You've got the kids that have access to guns, that see drugs sold on a daily basis. . . . If it happened [there], everybody would have said, "Did you hear what happened?" It would have been a big thing, but it wouldn't have been an attorney's son from Heath. People move out to Heath to put their kids in school so they don't go to the city school.

Media pundits weighed in on the causes of deadly school shootings, and academic studies, government commissions, congressional working groups, and presidential summits soon followed—too many, some argued, given how seldom school shootings happen. Indeed, critics such as Orlando Patterson, a sociologist, and Michael Eric Dyson, a professor of African-American studies, argued that the only reason these rare events generated the attention they did was that the shooters and most of the victims were white. Had they been black, the attention would have been minimal and the need to explain the pathology less pronounced.

Models derived from the study of urban violence have minimal value in deciphering the causes of rampage school shootings.

There are good reasons to dwell on rampage school shootings even though they are rare. They are an unprecedented kind of adolescent violence. We do not understand why they happen and have barely begun to consider their long-term consequences. Models derived from the study of urban violence have minimal value in deciphering the causes of rampage school shootings. Understanding what leads to these attacks does not free anyone of the obligation to think just as hard about the far more common incidence of urban shootings, something social scientists and policymakers have been working on for decades. . . .

Epidemic or "Schoolhouse Hype"?

In the year following the massacre at Columbine High School, the nation's fifty largest newspapers printed nearly 10,000 stories related to the event and its aftermath, averaging about one story per newspaper every other day. No wonder parents worried about their children. A Gallup poll conducted in August 2000 found that 26 percent of American parents feared for their children's safety at school. Twenty-nine percent of the high school students polled by ABC News in March 2001 said that they saw some risk of an attack at their school, but immediately after the Columbine attack, 40 percent saw some risk.

The intense media coverage and renewed fear generated by the string of shootings around the country led some observers to claim that we are in the midst of an epidemic. This view has not gone unchallenged. Critics, such as the Justice Policy Institute, have argued that the widespread "panic" over school shootings is unjustified. In reports issued in July 1998 and April 2000, the institute reminded the nation that school is still the safest place for a child to be. Even during the seemingly deadly 1998–1999 school year, the chances of dying in school from homicide or suicide were less than one in 2 million. The rate of *out-of-school* homicides alone was about forty times higher.

Schools are indeed the safest place for our children to be, statistically. Yet if parents and children fear school violence, the schools' primary mission will be profoundly impaired.

What worried opponents of the epidemic hypothesis was not just the hype but the responses emerging from policymakers. Resources that might be spent on addressing more deadly problems facing America's youth, especially abuse, neglect, and inner-city youth violence, could be wasted on the statistically minor threat of school shootings. In the rush to take action, critics warned, educators might adopt measures that could backfire, including zero-tolerance policies, profiling, or security measures that induce or aggravate a climate of fear or shunt more troubled youths into the criminal justice system. Finally, they feared that intense media coverage of school shootings would spark more violence as copycats swung into action.

Both perspectives, the epidemic view and the hype view, have some merit. Schools are indeed the safest place for our children to be, statistically. Yet if parents and children fear school violence, the schools' primary mission will be profoundly impaired. Parents' concerns cannot be dismissed as irrelevant just because they are not entirely rational.

A New Kind of Violence

Moreover, their fears are not unfounded. Attacks . . . *did* increase in the 1990s. They are assaults of a very specific kind, and it pays to bear their characteristics in mind. As we define them, rampage school shootings must:

- take place on a school-related public stage before an audience;

- involve multiple victims, some of whom are shot simply for their symbolic significance or at random; and

- involve one or more shooters who are students or former students of the school.

This definition excludes many kinds of shootings that are cause for worry as well. For example, a student who comes to school looking to shoot a particular antagonist, or the school principal, but does not fire at others would not be counted here. Gang violence, revenge killings following drug deals that go bad—these kinds of mayhem are not included in our definition. Rampage school shootings, then, are a subset of a much larger category of murders or attempted murders and are closer in form to workplace or "postal" attacks than they are to single-victim homicides on or off campus.

Bearing this definition in mind, we can now turn our attention to the patterns that have emerged in recent years. . . . The numbers are very low until the early 1990s. They began to increase in the 1992–1993 school year, peaking in 1997–1998 and falling again to zero in 2001–2002. Do these data reflect a short-term epidemic, squashed—as so many patterns were—by the enormous wound of the terrorist attacks on September 11, 2001? Possibly, but the story is not a simple one, because although the number of actual attacks declined, police and school officials foiled a number of plots in 2001–2002. . . . There is no way to know whether these plots would have culminated in shootings and deaths or would have stopped short, remaining nothing more than adolescent fantasies. Either way, they are not particularly reassuring: students are still thinking about, planning, and moving to execute rampage shootings.

Students are still thinking about, planning, and moving to execute rampage shootings.

Rampage shootings are not unique to the United States. At least five multiple-victim, student-perpetrated incidents of school violence have taken place in other nations since 1975—two in Canada, one in Germany, one in the Netherlands, and one in Kenya. Erfurt, Germany, was the unhappy scene of a sixth deadly attack in April 2002, in which a student who had been expelled from his high school returned in a fury and murdered sixteen people and wounded six. And although no rampage shootings occurred on middle or high school campuses after the September 11 terrorist attacks, several very similar shootings erupted on university campuses.

Curiously, the peak in school shootings came at a time when other trend lines for violence were headed in the opposite direction. Decreases were recorded in adult homicides, youth homicides, drug- and gang-related youth homicide in the inner cities, and nonlethal violence in schools for the same period when school shootings spiked. Of course, it must be remembered that this sharp uptick still represents a small number of deaths and that the incidence of homicide on school campuses remains low.

A poll taken in November 2001 revealed that 61 percent of high school students who knew of someone bringing a gun to school did not report it.

Media coverage does contribute to a school violence panic and certainly aggravates the difficulties for communities in which rampage episodes have occurred. But the press should also be credited with helping to avert some potential rampages. Articles pointing to the unwillingness of students to come forward when they heard warnings of impending violence trained attention on the need for teenagers to speak out and helped foil some near-miss plots. For example, in November 2001 a plot to shoot up a New Bedford, Massachusetts, high school was uncovered solely because one seventeen-year-old participant came forward.

Unfortunately, relaying threats to adults is not the norm. A poll taken in November 2001 revealed that 61 percent of high school students who knew of someone bringing a gun to school did not report it; 56 percent of those who heard another student make a weapons-related threat said nothing. Even so, between 1999 and 2001, at least seven school shootings were prevented when peers reported the plans to school or law enforcement authorities. The media coverage helped to shift the balance, at least in these cases.

2

The Media Exaggerate the School-Shooting Problem

Joel Best

Joel Best, professor of sociology and criminal justice at the University of Delaware, is the author of More Damned Lies and Statistics: How Numbers Confuse Public Issues.

In the late 1990s the media took a few isolated school-shooting incidents and made them into a national crisis. The media combined graphic images of injured children and statistics from poorly designed studies to exaggerate the seriousness of the school-shooting problem. One study, which claimed bullying was a primary factor in school shootings, defined bullying too broadly and did not distinguish between victims and perpetrators. Such studies represent bullying as a widespread phenomenon, generating unwarranted panic and draconian policies. Indeed, other studies have shown that levels of youth violence have actually been decreasing in recent years. Using graphic images and misleading studies, the media has created a social problem that does not exist.

Contemporary discussions about social issues, especially within education, almost always involve statistics. Numbers have become an essential element in policy rhetoric, a form of evidence needed to persuade others. Statistics let us

Joel Best, "Monster Hype: How a Few Isolated Tragedies—and Their Supposed Causes—Were Turned into a National 'Epidemic,'" *Education Next,* Summer 2002, p. 51. Copyright © 2002 by the Hoover Institution Press. Reproduced by permission.

claim that we can measure the size of our problems and the effectiveness of our solutions.

Nearly every [school] shooting was accompanied by reports that the teenagers involved were marginalized in some way.

Yet even as we rely on numbers, we are bedeviled by innumeracy, the mathematical equivalent of illiteracy. Too often, we fail to think critically about the statistics we encounter, to ask even the most basic questions. This is important, because accepting numbers uncritically may cause us to badly misunderstand our problems. There are few better examples of this failing than some of the recent figures regarding school violence.

Looking for Answers

The March 5, 2001, shooting spree at Santana High School in Santee, California, which left 2 dead and 13 injured, revived concerns over the seeming escalation of school violence and its potential links to the age-old schoolyard tradition of bullying. School shootings first became a serious issue in the wake of a series of tragic incidents, the most famous being Dylan Klebold and Eric Harris's April 1999 rampage at Columbine High School, in Littleton, Colorado, during which they murdered 12 students and a teacher before turning their weapons on themselves. Of particular interest was that nearly every shooting was accompanied by reports that the teenagers involved were marginalized in some way; the Santee shooter especially appears to have been a victim of bullying.

Both school shootings and bullying have become subjects of extensive media coverage, featuring the pontification of assorted politicians, activists, and experts. This is how contemporary Americans create new social problems. Typically, the process involves a three-part recipe:

1. Illustrate the problem with an awful example (e.g., the mass murder at Columbine High School).
2. Give the problem a name ("school shootings").
3. Use statistics to suggest the problem's size and importance.

Statistics play a crucial role in this process, because we tend to assume that numbers are factual—that somebody has counted something, that the problem has been measured and therefore is as big as the claims suggest. Coupled with dramatic, headline-grabbing incidents, they have created the impression that both school violence and bullying are on the rise. This may make for compelling television, but the oversaturated media coverage can portray a few isolated incidents as a national trend. Take CBS anchor Dan Rather's post-Santee warning: "School shootings in this country have become an epidemic." Such claims have become commonplace among journalists who haven't thought carefully enough about the evidence. The statistics on violence and bullying that are trucked out by pundits and activists often exaggerate or distort the case. The result is that the public and policymakers tend to overreact as they look for solutions to problems that appear to be out of control. A closer look at the statistics, however, reveals a more complicated and hopeful picture.

A Phantom Epidemic

Of course, the phenomenon of adolescents' bringing guns to school and randomly shooting their peers ought to be a source of genuine worry. The 1997–98 school year alone saw tragedy strike West Paducah, Kentucky (3 dead, 5 more wounded); Jonesboro, Arkansas (5 dead, 10 wounded); and Springfield, Oregon (2 deaths and 21 wounded at the school, after the shooter first killed his parents at home). These crimes, along with the Columbine massacre, seemed to be without rational motivation; what could possibly have driven these adolescents to lash out at the world in such bloody fashion? Kids have always divided into cliques and subjected the nonconforming to verbal and physical abuse; only recently, it seemed, had the social drama of high school resulted in mass casualties. It's legitimate to wonder whether these incidents represent a deep-seated change in youth culture.

Nevertheless, these tragic events masked the overall trend: a good deal of evidence indicates that school violence has actually been declining in recent years. When researchers at the National School Safety Center (NSSC) combed media reports from the school years 1992–93 to 2000–01, they identified 321 violent deaths at school. However, not all of these incidents involved student-on-student violence: they included, for example, 16 accidental deaths and 56 suicides, as well as incidents involving nonstudents, such as a teacher killed by her estranged husband, who then shot himself, and a nonstudent killed on a school playground during the weekend. Even if we include all 321 deaths, the average fell from 48 violent deaths per year during the school years 1992–93 through 1996–97 to 32 per year from 1997–98 to 2000–01. If accidental deaths and suicides are eliminated from the data, the decline remains: from an average of 31 deaths per year in the earlier period to 24 per year in the later one. Moreover, the later period includes all of the heavily publicized cases mentioned above. And the later figure may be further inflated by the likelihood that the media were more apt to report school shootings after the topic vaulted to public attention.

Oversaturated media coverage can portray a few isolated incidents as a national trend.

This decline is consistent with the evidence suggesting that crime rates were declining nationwide, During the 1990s, the overall crime rate fell, as did the rates of major violent crimes such as homicide, robbery, and aggravated assault. The crime rate, which is the Federal Bureau of Investigation's tally of crimes reported to the police, is only one of two national measures of criminal activity. The second, less familiar measure is the rate of victimization reported in the National Crime Victimization Survey. Researchers with the victimization survey interview a large national sample and ask respondents whether they or anyone in their households have been victims of crime. This survey showed instances of criminal victimization falling during the 1990s. Moreover, reports of teenagers being victimized by violent crimes at school dropped. The data also showed that instances of victimization were less common at school than elsewhere; in other words, teenagers were safer at school.

The federal Centers for Disease Control and Prevention's Youth Risk Behavior Survey also found steadily declining percentages of high-school students who reported fighting or carrying weapons on school property during the 1990s. It is also important to recognize that the risks of school violence are extremely low. For every million children who attend school, there is less than one violent school-related death per year. Moreover, only about 1 percent of children killed by violence are hurt at school, despite the large amount of time they spend there.

These tragic events masked the overall trend: a good deal of evidence indicates that school violence has actually been declining in recent years.

None of these data are especially hard to come by; all of them were readily available—and the trends they showed were apparent—before, during, and after the various school-shooting incidents that became subjects of extensive news coverage. All of this evidence flatly contradicted the claims that there was a wave, trend, or epidemic of school violence. In other words, the wave of school shootings was a phantom—that is, a nonexistent trend. What accounts for this misperception? Why did the press and the public assume that school shootings were increasing?

A Distorted Picture

In large part, media coverage promoted this distorted view of the problem. The Columbine killings in particular became a huge story. Columbine involved many victims, and the story unfolded over hours. Because the crime occurred in the suburbs of a major city, there were plenty of reporters nearby, and they had time to arrive on the scene for live coverage. The result was dramatic video footage that would be replayed many times. Furthermore, Columbine was a bastion of suburban privilege; it challenged stereotypes about inner-city violence. It was a story made for television.

The problem with trying to measure the extent of schoolyard bullying should be obvious: the term lacks any clear definition.

The Columbine coverage also reflected recent media transformations. Most Americans now have access to cable or satellite television systems; they are no longer limited to receiving broadcasts from a handful of local stations. Most viewers now can choose among several all-news or public-affairs channels. Those channels need constantly to fill the time with content. In the aftermath of the Columbine shootings, broadcasters like CNN, Fox News, and MSNBC devoted hours, not just to reporting the story and commentary about the violence, but also to live coverage of many funeral and memorial services. Columbine remained a major story for days, and during that period, politicians, activists, and commentators used it as evidence to justify their calls for a wide range of measures, including tougher gun laws, restrictions on adolescents' access to violent popular culture, and so on.

The Columbine killings were a terrible event, but we are accustomed to thinking about such incidents as instances— that is, as examples of some larger problem. The extraordinary level of media coverage reinforced the interpretation that these killings must have had some larger significance. It also gave people the sense that school shootings must be a large and growing problem, regardless of what the available statistics actually showed.

Making Bullies Seem Big

Concern with school bullying usually concentrates on mundane, everyday cruelty, but the issue has taken on new significance with reports that several school shooters were reacting to a history of taunts and shoves from their peers. All of us have witnessed—if not experienced—bullying, usually during our own school days. The phenomenon has long been recognized as undermining efforts to maintain discipline in schools.

The problem with trying to measure the extent of schoolyard bullying should be obvious: the term lacks any clear definition. What is bullying? Any attempt to measure bullying requires not just defining bullying in the abstract, but also devising an operational definition—that is, a set of procedures or operations whereby one can identify and count cases of bullying. In general, those who are trying to provoke a policy response to a particular social problem favor broad, inclusive definitions. Their purpose is to make the problem seem as widespread as possible. If bullying is defined narrowly—say, as involving only physical assaults—it will seem like less of a problem than if the definition includes many other forms of hurtful behavior.

Why Definitions Are Important

Consider "Bullying Behaviors Among U.S. Youth," an article published in the April 25, 2001, issue of the *Journal of the American Medical Association (JAMA)*. The article reported results from a large (nearly 16,000 respondents) representative sample of students in grades 6 through 10; the authors were associated with the National Institute of Child Health and Human Development (which supported the survey). Its major finding, widely reported by the media, was that nearly 30 percent of youths "reported moderate or frequent involvement in bullying." This was just one of many studies of bullying, but few other studies feature samples as large and well drawn. In addition, this article appeared in *JAMA,* an especially prestigious journal, so we might assume that it represents the best work on bullying. Nevertheless, it is hard to imagine *JAMA* finding the space to publish these results if the researchers had found that only 3 percent of youths were involved in bullying, let alone to picture the news media heralding the article's publication.

The authors [of one study] made a series of choices that allowed them to estimate that bullying significantly affects 30 percent of students; different choices . . . would have produced a figure that was perhaps a quarter as large.

Of course, the proportion of surveyed students who report being involved in bullying will depend on how bullying is defined and how the questions are framed. The questionnaire's section on bullying began with an explanation: "Here are some questions about bullying. We say a student is *being bullied* when another student, or a group of students, say or do nasty and unpleasant things to him or her. It is also bullying when a student is teased repeatedly in a way he or she doesn't like. But it is *not bullying* when two students of about the same strength quarrel or fight." The students were then asked how frequently they bullied others or were bullied during the current school term. They had to choose from the following responses: "I haven't . . . ," "once or twice," "sometimes," "about once a week," or "several times a week." In presenting their results, the authors defined incidents that occurred at least weekly as frequent involvement in bullying, and responses of "sometimes" as moderate involvement.

The authors conclude that "bullying is a serious problem for U.S. youth," and that "the prevalence of bullying observed in this study suggests the importance of preventive intervention research targeting bullying behaviors." But the data are much less clear than these conclusions suggest. The central finding—that 30 percent of youths are involved in bullying— depends on three manipulations, three methodological choices. First, students could be involved either as a bully (13 percent), as a victim (11 percent), or as both (6 percent). If the article's authors had chosen to count only the victims, they would have found that 17 percent, rather than 30 percent, were subject to bullying. Second, the authors included both "moderate" bullying (those who reported bullying as occurring "sometimes"—more than once or twice during the term, but less than weekly), and "frequent" bullying (occurring at least weekly). Adopting a narrower definition would have made the findings less dramatic; only 8 percent of the respondents reported being targets of frequent bullying. Third, there were separate questions about bullying in and out of school, but those responses were combined for the *JAMA* article, so readers are not told how much of the reported bullying actually occurred in schools. We can assume that at least some of the students who reported being frequently bullied were targeted outside of school. If so, the percentage of students who reported frequent bullying in school should have been even lower than 8 percent.

In other words, the authors made a series of choices that allowed them to estimate that bullying significantly affects 30 percent of students; different choices—say, looking only at victims of frequent bullying in schools—would have produced a figure that was perhaps a quarter as large. The point is not that this is a bad piece of research, nor that bullying can't have serious consequences (remember the Santee shooter). Rather, it is that the numbers that emerge from social-science research need to be handled with some care. How the survey's questions were worded, the order in which they were asked, and the choices made in interpreting and summarizing the data for publication all shaped the results.

Why Statistics Matter

Most of us depend on statistics; we need them to summarize our world, which is otherwise too large and complex to grasp. We equate numbers with facts, and figures have become an essential element in contemporary policy discussions. They are used to document the existence, size, and other dimensions of social problems. Still, even though we depend upon statistics, we need to view them critically. Statistics are not little nuggets of truth. Rather, they are products of someone's efforts. Any number means that someone has gone to the trouble of counting something. This raises questions: Who did the counting, and why? What did they count? How did they go about counting it? Why did they choose to count what they did, and to go about it in the way they did?

Perceptions that school violence is a national crisis have clearly affected educational policy. Resources have been directed toward purchasing and operating metal detectors, stationing police officers in schools, and enhancing other security measures, restrictions that many schools expanded in the aftermath of the September 11 terrorist attacks. These are not necessarily bad choices, but they may have been based in part on inaccurate perceptions of the nature and level of school violence.

3

Violent Video Games Train School Shooters

Jack Thompson

Attorney Jack Thompson represented the families of three girls who were victims of a school shooting in Paducah, Kentucky, in December 1997. He speaks and writes frequently about violent video game entertainment and copycat violence.

Many video games sold to the general public, including Metal Gear Solid 2 *and* Full Spectrum Warrior, *were originally developed by the military to be used for sniper training. One effect of these games is to suppress the natural inhibition to kill. The FBI and the U.S. Secret Service contend that intense engagement with these violent video games is a factor in numerous school shootings. In fact, killing simulation games have been found in the homes of most school shooters who use these games to prepare for attacks on their classmates.*

NBC's *Today* host, Matt Lauer, asked me two weeks before John Allen Muhammad and Lee Boyd Malvo were identified and caught, "Who do you think the Beltway Sniper is?" I told the audience, "We will find it is a teen-age boy trained on a shooter video game switched to 'God mode.' 'I am God' on the tarot card—a gamer mantra—is a clue."

Two months later, *Dateline NBC* reported that Muhammad had Malvo "train on the Microsoft XBox game *Halo* switched to 'God-mode' to suppress his inhibition to kill and it worked." Malvo's Virginia prosecutor admitted there were witnesses to the *Halo* training.

On June 18, [2004,] a 12-year-old boy, dressed in camouflage, walked into his Bull Run Middle School in Prince William County, Va., armed with a rifle, a knife, butane fuel and 100 rounds of ammunition. He planned to take hostages, take over the school and settle scores. A passer-by heard the familiar sound of a gun being loaded as he walked by a bathroom, and a new "Columbine" was narrowly averted. "We were very, very lucky," said Prince William School Board Chairman Lucy Beauchamp. Indeed they were.

A Pattern Is Appearing

The Prince William County Police got a search warrant and seized guns and computer equipment in this commando wannabe's home, but they had missed something. Having represented the parents of the three girls shot and killed by 14-year-old Michael Carneal in the Paducah, Ky., school massacre, and having predicted Columbine on the *Today* show eight days before it happened, I called the Prince William Police and suggested they needed another search warrant—this one looking for violent video games. Why? Because the FBI and Secret Service found in the aftermath of Columbine that such violent entertainment invariably plays a role in such school shootings. Dozens of such incidents since Columbine have confirmed this.

Kids are training themselves on simulators, some of them created by [the Department of Defense,] to kill one another.

[In 2003,] an 11-year-old boy dressed in camouflage tried to take over his Wellsboro, Pa., middle school. He had obsessively trained on *Metal Gear Solid 2,* a commando game in which the hero wears a red bandanna. The Bull Run boy was sporting a red bandanna—a clue.

Prince William County Detective Tom Garrity, the lead detective in the Beltway snipers case and in this Bull Run case as well, called me and told me I was right in predicting killing simulation games would be found in a subsequent search of this boy's home. "We found 13 of them, including the commando games *Splinter Cell, Operation Wolf* and *Halo.* The Secret Service is analyzing the computer for more."

When I spoke by phone with the accused's father, I asked him if his son played commando killing games. "He played them too much, I am embarrassed to say. He played *Metal Gear Solid 2* on the computer. It was one of his favorite games," the father replied.

Killing Simulators Are Packaged as Games

The Department of Defense [DOD] has set up the Institute for Creative Technologies at the University of Southern California. DOD takes our tax dollars and pays the video-game industry to create virtual-reality-killing simulators—video games. DOD then frees the industry to sell these killing simulators on the civilian market. The latest installment of this desensitization subsidy is *Full Spectrum Warrior* made for DOD by Pandemic Studios. It's a top seller with kids across the country. . . .

It was reported there were 48 school-related violent deaths in America in the [2003–2004] academic year . . . up from 17 and 16 in the prior two years. "This is a pending crisis. We know it's coming—we can guarantee it's coming," said L.A. Police Chief William Bratton.

For 200 years, American kids went to school with guns to hunt after classes. They did not turn them on one another. What is different?

Here's a clue. Kids are training themselves on simulators, some of them created by DOD, to kill one another. Medical studies show kids process the games in a different part of the brain than do adults, the sector that leads to copycatting. Garbage in, garbage out.

You think Columbine was bad? Just wait.

4

Violent Video Games Do Not Create School Shooters

Henry Jenkins

Henry Jenkins is the director of the Comparative Media Studies Program at the Massachusetts Institute of Technology.

Video games do not make otherwise normal young people into school shooters. Despite the fact that most American kids play video games, violent juvenile crime is at a thirty-year low. Claims that violent video games lead to aggressive behavior misinterpret the evidence. Indeed, no research has shown that violent video games are the primary factor in school violence. Violence is part of human culture and is present in all the arts. When adults overreact to violent video games, they stigmatize kids who already feel isolated and fail to address the real causes of school violence.

A large gap exists between the public's perception of video games and what the research actually shows. The following is an attempt to separate fact from fiction.

Looking at the Evidence

The availability of video games has led to an epidemic of youth violence. According to federal crime statistics, the rate of juvenile violent crime in the United States is at a 30-year

Henry Jenkins, "Reality Bytes: Eight Myths About Video Games Debunked," www.pbs.com, June 11, 2005. Copyright © 2005 by Henry Jenkins. Reproduced by permission.

low. Researchers find that people serving time for violent crimes typically consume less media before committing their crimes than the average person in the general population. It's true that young offenders who have committed school shootings in America have also been game players. But young people in general are more likely to be gamers—90 percent of boys and 40 percent of girls play. The overwhelming majority of kids who play do not commit antisocial acts. According to a 2001 U.S. Surgeon General's report, the strongest risk factors for school shootings centered on mental stability and the quality of home life, not media exposure. The moral panic over violent video games is doubly harmful. It has led adult authorities to be more suspicious and hostile to many kids who already feel cut off from the system. It also misdirects energy away from eliminating the actual causes of youth violence and allows problems to continue to fester.

The overwhelming majority of kids who play [video games] do not commit antisocial acts.

Scientific evidence links violent game play with youth aggression. Claims like this are based on the work of researchers who represent one relatively narrow school of research, "media effects." This research includes some 300 studies of media violence. But most of those studies are inconclusive and many have been criticized on methodological grounds. In these studies, media images are removed from any narrative context. Subjects are asked to engage with content that they would not normally consume and may not understand. Finally, the laboratory context is radically different from the environments where games would normally be played. Most studies found a correlation, not a causal relationship, which means the research could simply show that aggressive people like aggressive entertainment. That's why the vague term "links" is used here. If there is a consensus emerging around this research, it is that violent video games may be one risk factor—when coupled with other more immediate, real-world influences—which can contribute to anti-social behavior. But no research has found that video games are a primary factor or that violent video game play could turn an otherwise normal person into a killer.

Who Is Playing?

Children are the primary market for video games. While most American kids do play video games, the center of the video game market has shifted older as the first generation of gamers continues to play into adulthood. Already 62 percent of the console market and 66 percent of the PC [personal computing] market is age 18 or older. The game industry caters to adult tastes. Meanwhile, a sizable number of parents ignore game ratings because they assume that games are for kids. One quarter of children ages 11 to 16 identify an M-Rated (Mature Content) game as among their favorites. Clearly, more should be done to restrict advertising and marketing that targets young consumers with mature content, and to educate parents about the media choices they are facing. But parents need to share some of the responsibility for making decisions about what is appropriate for their children. The news on this front is not all bad. The Federal Trade Commission has found that 83 percent of game purchases for underage consumers are made by parents or by parents and children together.

***

No research has found that video games are a primary factor [in youth violence] or that violent video game play could turn an otherwise normal person into a killer.

***

Almost no girls play computer games. Historically, the video game market has been predominantly male. However, the percentage of women playing games has steadily increased over the past decade. Women now slightly outnumber men playing Web-based games. Spurred by the belief that games were an important gateway into other kinds of digital literacy, efforts were made in the mid-90s to build games that appealed to girls. More recent games such as *The Sims* were huge cross-over successes that attracted many women who had never played games before. Given the historic imbalance in the game market (and among people working inside the game industry), the presence of sexist stereotyping in games is hardly surprising. Yet it's also important to note that female game characters are often portrayed as powerful and independent. In his book *Killing Monsters,* Gerard Jones argues that young girls often build upon these representations of strong women warriors as a means of building up their self-confidence in confronting challenges in their everyday lives.

The Military Uses of Games

Because games are used to train soldiers to kill, they have the same impact on the kids who play them. Former military psychologist and moral reformer David Grossman argues that because the military uses games in training (including, he claims, training soldiers to shoot and kill), the generation of young people who play such games are similarly being brutalized and conditioned to be aggressive in their everyday social interactions.

Grossman's model only works if:

- we remove training and education from a meaningful cultural context.

- we assume learners have no conscious goals and that they show no resistance to what they are being taught.

- we assume that they unwittingly apply what they learn in a fantasy environment to real world spaces.

The military uses games as part of a specific curriculum, with clearly defined goals, in a context where students actively want to learn and have a need for the information being transmitted. There are consequences for not mastering those skills. That being said, a growing body of research does suggest that games can enhance learning. In his recent book, *What Video Games Have to Teach Us About Learning and Literacy,* James Gee describes game players as active problem solvers who do not see mistakes as errors, but as opportunities for improvement. Players search for newer, better solutions to problems and challenges, he says. And they are encouraged to constantly form and test hypotheses. This research points to a fundamentally different model of how and what players learn from games.

A Form of Expression

Video games are not a meaningful form of expression. On April 19, 2002, U.S. District Judge Stephen N. Limbaugh Sr. ruled that video games do not convey ideas and thus enjoy no constitutional protection. As evidence, Saint Louis County presented the judge with videotaped excerpts from four games, all within a narrow range of genres, and all the subject of previous controversy. Overturning a similar decision in Indianapolis, Federal Court of Appeals Judge Richard Posner noted: "Violence has always been and remains a central interest of humankind and a recurrent, even obsessive theme of culture both high and low. It engages the interest of children from an early age, as anyone familiar with the classic fairy tales collected by Grimm, Andersen, and Perrault are aware." Posner adds, "To shield children right up to the age of 18 from exposure to violent descriptions and images would not only be quixotic, but deforming; it would leave them unequipped to cope with the world as we know it." Many early games were little more than shooting galleries where players were encouraged to blast everything that moved. Many current games are designed to be ethical testing grounds. They allow players to navigate an expansive and open-ended world, make their own choices and witness their consequences. *The Sims* designer

Will Wright argues that games are perhaps the only medium that allows us to experience guilt over the actions of fictional characters. In a movie, one can always pull back and condemn the character or the artist when they cross certain social boundaries. But in playing a game, we choose what happens to the characters. In the right circumstances, we can be encouraged to examine our own values by seeing how we behave within virtual space.

The Effect of Playing

Video game play is socially isolating. Much video game play is social. Almost 60 percent of frequent gamers play with friends. Thirty-three percent play with siblings and 25 percent play with spouses or parents. Even games designed for single players are often played socially, with one person giving advice to another holding a joystick. A growing number of games are designed for multiple players—for either cooperative play in the same space or online play with distributed players. Sociologist Talmadge Wright has logged many hours observing online communities interact with and react to violent video games, concluding that meta-gaming (conversation about game content) provides a context for thinking about rules and rule-breaking. In this way there are really two games taking place simultaneously: one, the explicit conflict and combat on the screen; the other, the implicit cooperation and comradeship between the players. Two players may be fighting to death on screen and growing closer as friends off screen. Social expectations are reaffirmed through the social contract governing play, even as they are symbolically cast aside within the transgressive fantasies represented onscreen.

Video game play is desensitizing. Classic studies of play behavior among primates suggest that apes make basic distinctions between play fighting and actual combat. In some circumstances, they seem to take pleasure wrestling and tousling with each other. In others, they might rip each other apart in mortal combat. Game designer and play theorist Eric Zimmerman describes the ways we understand play as distinctive from reality as entering the "magic circle." The same action—say, sweeping a floor—may take on different meanings in play (as in playing house) than in reality (housework). Play allows kids to express feelings and impulses that have to be carefully held in check in their real-world interactions. Media reformers argue that playing violent video games can cause a lack of empathy for real-world victims. Yet, a child who responds to a video game the same way he or she responds to a real-world tragedy could be showing symptoms of being severely emotionally disturbed. Here's where the media effects research, which often uses punching rubber dolls as a marker of real-world aggression, becomes problematic. The kid who is punching a toy designed for this purpose is still within the "magic circle" of play and understands her actions on those terms. Such research shows us only that violent play leads to more violent play.

5

Protecting Athletes Who Bully Other Students Promotes School Shootings

Gary K. Clabaugh and Alison A. Clabaugh

Gary K. Clabaugh is professor of education at La Salle University. Alison A. Clabaugh is a doctoral student in social psychology at Temple University.

In the months leading up to the Columbine High School shooting in 1999, athletes routinely bullied, intimidated, and sexually harassed their classmates. School administrators failed to stop the abuse, punish rule breakers, or disqualify guilty athletes. The school administration's tolerance of aggressive behavior on the part of a privileged group of athletes created an atmosphere of fear and powerlessness among the students, especially those who were labeled social outcasts. Rather than looking at the victims of this abuse as "bad apples," school administrators who are interested in preventing school shootings should identify and change practices that protect students who abuse their classmates.

While a few bad apples might spoil the barrel (filled with good fruit/people), a vinegar barrel will always transform sweet cucumbers into sour pickles—regardless of the best intentions, resilience, and genetic nature of the cucumbers.

So does it make more sense to spend resources to identify, isolate, and destroy bad apples or to understand how vinegar works . . . ?

—*Phillip Zimbardo*

It was 11:19 A.M. on April 20, 1999—Hitler's 110th birthday—when Eric Harris and Dylan Klebold opened fire at Columbine High School near Littleton, Colorado. Planning to kill most of the 400-plus students eating at the time, the pair planted two twenty-pound bombs in the school cafeteria. Then they waited outside the building, hoping to pick off blast survivors as they staggered out.

When the bombs failed to detonate, the pair stormed into the cafeteria and opened fire. Forty minutes later, twelve students and a teacher lay lifeless; another twenty-three students were wounded—many gravely. Harris and Klebold also were dead of self-inflicted gunshot wounds. Police worked into the next day to find and deactivate the thirty bombs the pair had planted throughout the school.

The FBI's Bad Apples

What set Harris and Klebold off? The FBI's team of psychiatrists and clinical psychologists, including a Michigan State University psychiatrist and Supervisory Special Agent Dwayne Fuselier, the FBI's chief Columbine investigator, and a clinical psychologist, assert that Harris killed because he was a "psychopath." Klebold, they say, was "hotheaded, depressive, suicidal," and under Harris's influence. The FBI experts are not claiming that Harris was delusional or out of touch with reality. They are asserting that he simply was a world-class hater out to punish humanity for its inexcusable inferiority.

Is the FBI correct? Was this horrific incident simply the evil spawn of a remorseless teenager with a world-class superiority complex and an angry, suicidal alter ego? . . .

What was the situation at Columbine before the massacre? Was this high school one of those vinegar-filled barrels that transform sweet cucumbers into sour pickles, or were Harris and Klebold bad apples who spoiled an otherwise wholesome barrel?

The Columbine Pickle Barrel

A painstaking investigative report by the *Washington Post* describes pre-massacre Columbine as filled with social vinegar. The high school was dominated by a "cult of the athlete." In this distorted environment, a coterie of favored jocks—who wore white hats to set themselves apart—consistently bullied, hazed, and sexually harassed their classmates while receiving preferential treatment from school authorities.

Was [the school shooting at Columbine High School] simply the evil spawn of a remorseless teenager with a world-class superiority complex and an angry, suicidal alter ego?

Other students hated the abuses of the "steroid poster boys" but could do little. A former student testified, "Pretty much everyone was scared to take them on; if you said anything, they'd come after you, too." Here is more of what the *Post* found was going on at Columbine:

- *Bullying was rampant and unchecked.* For instance, a father told *Post* reporters about two athletes mercilessly bullying his son, a Jew, in gym class. They sang songs about Hitler, pinned the youngster to the ground, did "body twisters" on him until he was black-and-blue, and even threatened to set him on fire. The father reported the bullying to the gym teacher, but it continued. When the father took his complaint to the guidance counselor, he said, he was told, "This stuff can happen." The outraged father had to complain to the school board to get relief for his son.

- *Athletes convicted of crimes were neither suspended*

from games nor expelled from school. The homecoming king, a star football player, was on parole for burglary yet still permitted to play. Columbine's state wrestling champ was allowed to compete despite being on court-ordered probation, and school officials did nothing when he regularly parked his $100,000 Hummer all day in a fifteen-minute parking space.

- *Sexual harassment by athletes was common and ignored.* For example, when a girl complained to her teacher that a football player was making lewd comments about her breasts in class, the teacher, also a football and wrestling coach, suggested she change her seat. When an athlete loudly made similar comments at a Columbine wrestling match, the girl complained to the coach. He suggested she move to the other side of the gym. Finally, the girl complained to a woman working at a concession stand, who called police. The next day a school administrator tried to persuade the girl's mother to drop the charges, telling her that pressing them would prevent the boy from playing football. When the youngster was found guilty, he still was permitted to play.

Does Fairness Matter?

How important were these injustices to Harris and Klebold? Did they care about them, or even know about them? They both knew and they cared. In fact, the *Post* reports that dozens of interviews and court records alike show that the pair's homicidal anger ". . . began with the injustices of the jocks."

They became convinced that favored athletes could get away with anything. For instance, a close friend reported that the pair saw a star athlete, in front of a teacher, forcefully shove his girlfriend into a locker. The teacher did nothing. Such injustices enraged Harris and Klebold. That's why, just before opening fire in the cafeteria, they demanded that all the jocks stand up. They planned to kill them first.

In sum, pre-massacre Columbine High seems to have been the kind of place that "will always transform sweet cucumbers into sour pickles."

The Prison Study

Now let's put the social situation at Columbine in still broader perspective by turning to a well-known experiment by the social psychologist Phillip Zimbardo (quoted earlier). He set up a simulated "prison" in a Stanford University basement, where a random sample of psychologically "normal" college students was assigned one of two roles: prisoner or guard.

The experimental setting was realistic. Prisoners actually were kept behind bars, made to wear uniforms, and identified only by their numbers, such as "Prisoner #12." The guards, who worked in eight-hour shifts, were given Mace, handcuffs, and billy clubs.

A coterie of favored jocks . . . consistently bullied, hazed, and sexually harassed their classmates while receiving preferential treatment from school authorities.

Professor Zimbardo planned to observe the participants' behavior systematically for two weeks in their new "roles" within the social context of his "prison." But he ended the study after only six days because students playing the roles of "guards" exhibited an escalating level of violence and abuse toward the "prisoners." Although an initial battery of psychological tests indicated no pathology among participants, it had taken only a few days for situational forces to overwhelm dispositional ones. As Zimbardo noted, "The Evil situation triumphed over Good people."

Zimbardo's "prison" resembles the *Post*'s description of Columbine High. The favored clique of white-capped athletes assumed a role similar to that of Zimbardo's "guards." The outcasts, the kids who did not fit in, were their "prisoners." The abuse was essentially the same. Unlike the experiment, however, no one stepped in to end the intolerable situation at Columbine before it was too late.

Vinegar at Work

The fact that Harris and Klebold were social outcasts made them especially conspicuous targets for abuse. Social psychological research reveals that not fitting in is costly. Group members typically first try to persuade those holding minority opinions or who are otherwise different to conform to group standards. But if individuals still fail to conform, social rejection follows: nonconformists typically are ostracized as social pariahs.

That is precisely what happened to Harris and Klebold. Both notorious nonconformists, they definitely did not fit in. As one Columbine student observed, "They didn't look like other people," and "They didn't dress or act like other people." Consequently, they became social outcasts and victims, deeply resentful of their marginality and outraged by their subsequent victimization.

Educators charged with containing school violence . . . must discover and modify its causal networks.

Harris and Klebold were peripheral members of just one group: the so-called "Trench Coat Mafia." (The leading athletes assigned this name to a loose collection of the school's non-athletic social outcasts who had taken to wearing black— most markedly long black—trench coats.) Predictably, the athletes regarded these conspicuous rebels as especially legitimate targets for abuse, and Harris and Klebold got more than their share. Once, for instance, they were standing outside the school with a friend when a carload of athletes went by and a passenger threw a bottle at them. It smashed at their feet. The friend recalls Klebold saying, "Don't worry, man, it happens all the time."

Harris and Klebold's marginalization and subsequent maltreatment were major factors in the massacre. Their powerlessness in the face of this favored clique's illegitimate authority, psychological abuse, physical intimidation, and sexual harassment sparked a profound desire for revenge. As one student told a *Post* reporter, "They just let the jocks get to them. I think they were taunted to their limits."

Eventually their rage led to a plan to strike back at their tormentors. That, in turn, morphed into a scheme for indiscriminate mass murder in a school they had come to loathe.

Discovering and Modifying Causal Networks

None of our exploration is meant to excuse Harris or Klebold. As Zimbardo observes,

> Acknowledging the power of situational forces does not excuse the behaviors channeled by their operation. Rather, it provides a knowledge base to shift attention away from simplistic "blaming of the victim," and ineffective individualistic treatments designed to change the evildoer, toward more profound attempts to discover causal networks that should be modified.

That is the primary task of educators charged with containing school violence. They must discover and modify its causal networks. Years ago a pioneer social psychologist, Solomon Asch, incisively observed, "Most social acts have to be understood in their setting, and lose meaning if isolated. No error in thinking about social facts is more serious than the failure to see their place and function." Nevertheless, that is precisely the blunder the FBI fell into.

No matter how seductive they might seem, it is generally unwise to trust bad-apple explanations of school violence.

6

Antidepressants May Trigger School Shootings

Kelly Patricia O'Meara

A former chief of staff for the U.S. House of Representatives, Kelly Patricia O'Meara is an investigative reporter for Insight on the News.

Many experts claim that antidepressant medications can cause adverse reactions that may trigger school shootings. Indeed, a number of school shooters were taking antidepressant medications at the time of the shootings. Mark Taylor, a Columbine High School student who was shot between seven and thirteen times by Columbine High School shooter Eric Harris, filed suit against the manufacturer of the antidepressant Luvox. Taylor believes that Harris would not have gone on his shooting rampage in 1999 had he not been under the influence of the drug. Luvox is a member of a class of drugs called selective serotonin reuptake inhibitors (SSRIs) that have been associated with psychotic reactions and seizures. Taylor claims that the drug's manufacturer failed to provide adequate warning that it could cause psychotic reactions. The drug company settled the suit in 2003 by making a $10,000 donation to the American Cancer Society.

The kid spoke unsteadily: "I was sitting on a hill outside the school eating lunch with my best friend when Eric Harris came over and started shooting me. I was shot between seven and 13 times. No one really knows the exact number because there were so many bullet tracks. Most of the bullets just went right through me. After I was shot I just lay there, playing dead, and could see others being shot."

These are the recollections of 19-year-old Mark Taylor, who spent nearly two months in the hospital and has endured three years of follow-up operations for the gunshot wounds he received during the murderous 1999 rampage of Eric Harris and Dylan Klebold at Columbine High School in Littleton, Colo.

An Injured Student Sues Drug Company

Taylor slowly is recovering from his wounds and, in an effort to bring attention to what he believes was the cause of Harris' deadly rage, has filed a lawsuit against Solvay Pharmaceuticals Inc., the manufacturer of Luvox (Fluvoxamine), the antidepressant that Harris had been prescribed and was taking at the time of the shooting spree. Despite the deadly assault against him, Taylor's perception of the young men who nearly killed him is surprising.

"I'm suing Solvay because I believe that Eric Harris did what he did because of this drug" [says Taylor]. "I didn't personally know Eric, but I knew him as one of the 'Trench Coat Mafia.' Everybody thought Eric and Dylan were the nicest people. My cousin, who was in Eric's class, told me that Eric and Dylan used to bring her flowers and cookies. Eric was forced onto these drugs and I feel sorry for him, like so many other kids who are put on these drugs. I don't have ill feelings against him since I don't think you can hold him accountable, because he didn't know what he was doing." Taylor's lawsuit against Solvay claims that the mindaltering drug Luvox was the cause of Harris' rampage—that the drug made Harris manic and psychotic.

Luvox is in a class of antidepressants called selective serotonin reuptake inhibitors (SSRIs) that interact with the serotonergic system in the brain, as do Prozac, Zoloft and Paxil. Street drugs that interact with the serotonergic system include LSD and Ecstasy. The Food and Drug Administration approved Luvox in 1997 for treatment of obsessive-compulsive disorder in children, but not for treatment of depression.

Side Effects of the Drug Include Psychosis

The *Physicians Desk Reference* (PDR) records that, during controlled clinical trials of Luvox, manic reactions developed in 4 percent of children. Mania is defined as "a form of psychosis characterized by exalted feelings, delusions of grandeur . . . and overproduction of ideas." Court records show that the prescription for Harris had been filled 10 times between April 1998 and March 1999, and that three-and-a-half months before the shooting the dose had been increased—a common thread many experts say they are finding prior to adverse reactions to psychotropic drugs. The autopsy on Harris revealed a "therapeutic level" of Luvox in his system.

> *There is no doubt in my mind that [the antidepressant] Luvox caused [Columbine school shooter] Eric Harris to commit these acts.*

Other school shooters on antidepressants at the time of their attacks include 15-year-old Kip Kinkel who, while on Prozac, killed his parents and then proceeded to school where he opened fire on classmates, killing two and wounding 22 others; 14-year-old Elizabeth Bush, on "antidepressants" when she wounded one student at Bishop Neumann High School in

Williamsport, Pa.; and 18-year-old Jason Hoffman, on Effexor and Celexa when he wounded one teacher and three students at Granite Hills High School in El Cajon, Calif.

The medical histories of scores of "school shooters" have not been revealed; allegedly to protect the minor child. Ann Blake Tracy is a consultant in Taylor's lawsuit and director of the International Coalition for Drug Awareness. She holds a doctorate in biological psychology and is a specialist in what she believes are the adverse reactions to SSRI medications. She says Luvox caused Harris to go on the Columbine shooting spree and thinks the medical history of children who commit violent acts in school should be made public.

The Shooter Had a Bad Drug Reaction

"Suing Solvay for the injuries Mark Taylor suffered is one of the biggest SSRI suits we'll ever see," Tracy says. "It's a pivotal case because what happened at Columbine was so big. It's really crazy when you think about it. All you have to do is read the Luvox package insert to see that Eric's actions were due to an adverse reaction to this drug. Show me a drug anywhere that has listed mania and psychosis as frequent adverse reactions. That is what the insert says for Luvox. There is no doubt in my mind that Luvox caused Eric Harris to commit these acts."

The *PDR* lists adverse reactions of Luvox to the nervous system as:

> "*Frequent:* amnesia, apathy, hyperkinesis, hypokinesis, manic reaction, myoclonus, psychotic reaction;
>
> "*Infrequent:* agoraphobia, akathisia, CNS depression, convulsion, delirium, delusion, depersonalization, drug dependence, emotional liability, euphoria, hallucinations, hostility, hysteria, incoordination, increased salivation, increased libido, paralysis, paranoid reaction, phobia, psychosis, sleep disorder, stupor, twitching, vertigo."

Anger Management Problems
Were a Clue

Tracy continues, "Beyond the adverse reactions listed about Luvox, one of the first clues I had that these boys were on antidepressants was when it was made public that Eric [Harris] and Dylan Klebold had both been in anger-management classes. Anger-management classes equal antidepressants. Unfortunately, Dylan Klebold's medical records have been sealed, so there's no way of knowing what if anything he was on, but it makes sense that if he was in anger-management classes he was prescribed some antidepressant."

The problem, Tracy concludes, "is that this is a public-safety issue. So why is everything kept so secret, under lock and key? This information should be made available to the public so that people can learn from it and maybe we can stop this kind of tragedy from happening in the future. We've got a nightmare on our hands with these drugs, an absolute nightmare. We've got kids on these drugs that are ticking time bombs in every school in America. Most of these drugs are not approved for children, but it doesn't stop doctors from prescribing them. Laws should be passed requiring that this medical information be made public. And states should demand toxicology reports for drugs of this kind in all murders and suicides."

We've got kids on these [antidepressant] drugs that are ticking time bombs in every school in America.

Donald Marks specializes in internal medicine, has a doctorate in microbiology and has worked in pharmaceutical research for more than a decade in the area of drug safety and clinical research. Marks was brought into the Solvay lawsuit as an expert by Taylor and is not surprised that there may be a causal relationship between Luvox and Harris' murderous behavior. Marks also testified in a Wyoming case [in 2001] involving a murder related to the SSRI Paxil in which the defendant won an $8 million judgment against GlaxoSmithKline, maker of Paxil.

As part of the Columbine lawsuit, Taylor claims that Solvay failed to warn adequately of the risks and adverse reactions associated with Luvox, and Marks provides a preliminary expert opinion to the court stating that Solvay "acted in an unreasonable manner" by failing to provide adequate warnings of the adverse reactions to the drug. The Marks opinion continues: "In view of the evidence of a strong and likely causal relationship between SSRI medications, of which Luvox is one, and akathisia/suicide/homicide, Solvay should only have marketed this drug with prominent warnings and cautionary statements."

Important Information Was Not Shared

U.S. District Court Judge Clarence Brimmer has accepted Marks' preliminary report, allowing the case to go forward and giving the expert access to information that has been held under lock and key in a vault in Denver since the Columbine shooting. . . . "The preliminary report was based on what I know from past cases, because I haven't been allowed to examine information about Mr. Harris or anyone who knew him. The information has been locked in a room in Denver, and I haven't been allowed in the room until now" [says Marks].

According to Marks, "The real problem is that physicians, of which I am one, are not told that there is a potential for a causal relationship between these drugs and homicide and suicide. Therefore we're not educated to look for the kinds of adverse reactions that could herald this kind of event. That's why proper warnings about such drugs are so essential. I'm in the process of updating my report for the court, but my preliminary impression from looking at the material is that there very well could be a causal relationship here, that this drug could have been a factor that tipped Harris from being a troubled teen to a murderer."

Marks says, "In the report, I talk about the adverse-event profiles of other SSRI medications and how, in the context of rules of evidence, a statement of general causation could be made for all SSRI medications and how it could be applied to Luvox. The neuro-psychiatric-event profiles of the SSRI drugs are clearly associated with seizures and psychosis. Some have been associated with hypoglycemia, suicide and homicide. So it's not entirely implausible that one additional member of this class, like Luvox, would have those same effects."

The real problem is that physicians . . . are not told that there is a potential for a causal relationship between these [antidepressant] drugs and homicide and suicide.

The fact that the court has allowed the case to go forward is a good sign for Taylor, but there have been some very strange developments. Lincoln, Neb., attorney John DeCamp, who now represents Taylor against Solvay, [says] that "two days after I took the case, Solvay pulled Luvox from the market. I don't know if my coming on the case had any bearing on them pulling the drug, but it is interesting." Solvay announced that the drug was being removed temporarily from the U.S. market to revise data about how Luvox is manufactured.

Families of Victims Feared Losing Everything

Another interesting twist involves families pulling out of the lawsuit. "I am very reliably informed," DeCamp says, "and I'm satisfied that the people telling me this aren't lying, that at the settlement conference families were informed that a Colorado law that applies both in federal and state court says: 'If you lose, you pay.' These families were told that if they continued to sue and lost the case they would be sued in return and they'd lose their homes, cars and everything for the rest of their lives. So if you were one of these families what would you do?"

According to DeCamp, "My client is basically judgment-proof. In other words, Mark doesn't have anything. The other families didn't settle, they just dropped out of the suit—they were basically told that they were going to lose and, when it was over, the pharmaceutical companies were going to own their lives. It's fair to say that my client was presented with this argument, but he doesn't have anything."

The neuro-psychiatric-event profiles of the SSRI drugs . . . have been associated with hypoglycemia, suicide and homicide.

The lawyer continues, "It's also interesting in this case that there's more security to keep related evidence from surfacing than there is to get into the White House or Fort Knox. I have never, in 35 years practicing law, seen its like. There's been more evidence gathered than you can even imagine—things that I hope one day will be made public. I stated in court that if ever there was a monumental event this is it and the information that is locked in this room should be made public. History will be very unforgiving if that doesn't happen."

But the foremost question in the minds of experts on adverse reactions to SSRIs is whether history is just repeating itself. Recent court decisions, however, may be useful in Taylor's case against Solvay.

Other Drugs Have Caused Similar Reactions

In April 2001, then 16-year-old Cory Baadsgaard took a rifle to Wahluke High School in Washington State and took 23 classmates and a teacher hostage. Baadsgaard was held in jail for 14 months. Based on expert testimony by psychiatrists about the adverse reactions to the drugs he was taking, he finally was released from jail under community supervision for five years. Baadsgaard has no memory of his violent actions toward his classmates, which took place exactly 21 days after he had been cold-turkeyed off Paxil and switched to a high dose of Effexor (an SSRI) to treat "situational depression."

Cory's father, Jay Baadsgaard, says, "The morning that Cory went to school and did what he did, my wife and I just knew that it had to be something with the drugs. That morning he had taken about 300 milligrams of Effexor, and I thought it was something about him going off one of the drugs and then the high dose of the other. One of Cory's friends told us that Cory was yelling and then he just stopped, looked down and saw the gun in his hand and woke up."

There is no doubt that Cory is lucky not to have gone further, says his father, "and I guess I could blame myself for having the gun available, but if I'd known then just what these drugs could do it would have been the drugs that would not have been in our home. They always talk about how the kids who do these things are the ones who get picked on by the jocks and stuff, but Cory was a jock. He was on the varsity basketball team, played football and golf, and was very popular in school. I pray every night that the media will get ahold of this issue. If Cory had been on PCP the media would say 'Oh, he needs drug rehabilitation,' but because these were prescribed medications they say 'Oh, it can't be that,' but now we know it can be."

Taylor hopes his lawsuit against Solvay will make people aware of the dangerous side effects of such drugs. "Someone," he says, "has to do something about these drugs, because too many people are dying."

7

Teaching Boys to Solve Problems with Violence Promotes School Shootings

Seth Hicks

Seth Hicks is the male outreach coordinator for CARe, an initiative of Communities Against Rape.

People ignore one common factor when trying to explain school shootings: All the perpetrators have been boys. Society teaches boys that it is acceptable to use violence to gain power and control over others. While girls internalize their problems, boys are taught to solve their problems using violence. If society continues to condone male violence, it does so at the risk of more school shootings.

When I . . . read about the actions of Jeff Weise at Red Lake High School [where he killed a guard, a teacher, and five students], I felt like I was having a flashback. Again a heavily-armed high school student stalked the halls of his school with teachers and students fleeing in terror from a hail of bullets. Again multiple victims were brutally murdered and the perpetrator died from suicide as law enforcement arrived and began to respond.

The Same Story

Again the media report the same story. The perpetrator was a loner, a shy, withdrawn person. There was a history of alienation from peers and teachers at school. This time the media focused on some posts on a neo-Nazi Web discussion board. Most of the coverage . . . was composed of reporters trying furiously to hold up neo-Nazi-ism as a causal factor for what happened at Red Lake High. Previously, they have talked about trenchcoats, dressing "goth," the availability of guns, watching movies like "The Matrix," bullying, playing violent video games and other Internet usage.

All of these explanations for what has occurred have sounded to me like blind groping for an explanation. We are desperate to place a label on the perpetrators [that] will distance them from us. We want to know what causes this type of behavior. It would feel so comfortable and easy to blame this one on Hitler, the great demon of the late 20th century, or the Internet, the rising monster of the 21st.

All of the perpetrators of all of the school shootings in the last 15 years have been males.

The phenomenon of school shootings in the United States is beginning to read like a series of sick Mad Libs. The scripts are nearly identical with shy, victimized loners seizing power over their persecutors through gun violence. Fill in the blank. The perpetrator was a/an (a) goth, (b) overweight student, (c) neo-Nazi. Pick your letter and describe your multiple murder. All of the explanations we have plugged into the script seek to differentiate these killers as individuals, but ignore one critical common factor in their crimes.

A Common Factor

I have not used the words "he" or "his" in talking about the perpetrator so far in the Weise shootings. Neither have the media. With one exception: all of the perpetrators of all of the school shootings in the last 15 years have been males. No mainstream media have made this connection. If 99 percent of a variety of heinous violent crimes were committed by women or girls would they have noticed? You bet they would have.

The press would not have had space to get around to mentioning a few posts on a neo-Nazi Web site. Violence in boys, however, is accepted, expected and apparently not worthy of mention as a common feature in all these crimes.

Boys act out violently because we train them and arm them to do so both with actual guns and with the power and privilege of violent masculinity.

If guns were the cause, what has prevented female students from getting guns? It is their right to bear arms just as it is for males. Females' grandfathers have handguns and bulletproof vests, too. If video games are the cause, what causes boys to gravitate to violent video games in higher numbers? There is no gender requirement to purchase video games. If violent films contribute to these killings, why do we call "action" movies, which feature shootings, assaults, explosions and multiple murders, "guy" films? If bullying is the cause, why do the millions of young girls who are bullied daily in our schools not arm themselves and take revenge on their perceived persecutors? Why? Because solving your problems and taking control of others through violence is a skill taught to and reserved for men and boys.

How We Prepare Boys for Violence

We teach our boys from birth that they are entitled to this power. We then make and promote sports, movies and video games that remind boys of this entitlement and help develop their skills for using their power against others. When we are so generous in providing these skills to young boys, why does it surprise us so much when they use them to protect themselves from perceived attackers?

Access to weapons, bullying, Hitler and alienation of students are huge problems. These issues are experienced by girls all over the United States as well. We teach girls, however, to internalize their problems and suffer in silence through depression, anxiety, eating disorders and other "quiet" problems. Boys act out violently because we train them and arm them to do so both with actual guns and with the power and privilege of violent masculinity. This privilege normalizes and empowers men and boys to act out their feelings on others. It can be as little as shouts and punching lockers or it can be as much as the events at Red Lake High School. If we continue to ignore violent masculinity as a causal factor in school violence, we can expect to see more flashbacks to Columbine [High School where 12 students and one teacher were killed by Eric Harris and Dylan Klebold] and Red Lake in the future. The script will be the same.

8

Overreacting to School Shootings Intensifies the Problem

James Alan Fox and Jack Levin

James Alan Fox is a professor of criminal justice and Jack Levin is a professor of sociology and criminology at Northeastern University.

Overzealous efforts to reduce school shootings may simply intensify the fear of some students. Drawing attention to school shootings reminds others that violence is a way to solve their problems. Educators must instead address the causes of school violence—a disrespectful climate, bullying, and a lack of community—without drawing attention to violent behavior itself. Knowing students better and helping them to deal with their problems sooner is the best way to prevent future school shootings.

Although images of the 1999 Columbine [High School] massacre are still fresh in our minds, we appear to have turned the corner in the struggle to control school violence.

[At that time] it seemed as though there was no end in sight to the growing threat of schoolyard terror. Survey after survey indicated that school safety was the most critical issue for parents, well ahead of concerns over curriculum quality or the availability of educational resources.

Amidst a pervasive state of alarm, many administrators responded by turning their schools into armed camps. They upgraded security and sought to identify potentially violent students by scanning for warning signs such as black trenchcoats or bullying. More and more students passed through metal detectors and were repeatedly reminded to be on the lookout for anyone uttering a threat.

Oddly, well meaning efforts to reduce school shootings may actually have had the unintended effect of intensifying fear in vulnerable students while encouraging angry students to take up guns against their classmates. These practices inadvertently reminded vengeful students around the country about one particular way to resolve their problems. Violence against classmates had become, if not an accepted way, at least a familiar way to respond to classroom bullies. The attention we paid to school violence only reinforced that notion.

The Evolution of School Violence

While most children identify with the pain of the victims, a few alienated youngsters identify more with the power of the perpetrators. They see school shooters not as villains but as heroes. Not only did they get even with the nasty bullies and insensitive teachers, but they're famous for it.

Well meaning efforts to reduce school shootings may actually have had the unintended effect of intensifying fear in vulnerable students while encouraging angry students to take up guns against their classmates.

In many respects, the problems students face today are no different than earlier generations. There have been schoolyard bullies as long as there have been schools; there has been adolescent alienation as long as there have been teenagers.

Yet, earlier generations of disgruntled youngsters responded in less violent ways. School homicides committed by teenagers a decade ago were isolated cases of mostly one-on-one attacks. They didn't make the national news.

Do Not Reinforce the Symptoms

We are not suggesting that the problem of school violence be ignored. Rather, educators must learn to respond to a violent episode without gratuitously calling so much direct attention to it. We should focus on the causes of school violence—a disrespectful climate, large and impersonal schools and bullying—without continually reinforcing the symptoms.

The core problem at many schools is a lack of any sense of community. Too many students are nameless faces to teachers, psychologists and guidance counselors, whose huge caseloads in oversized schools do not permit them to know their students as individuals. If we really want to assess students for violent tendencies, we have to get to know them better. We should deal with the troubled student long before he or she becomes troublesome.

Examining the Cause and Effect

Why then the sudden drop in episodes of school shootings since Columbine? Could it be that our security efforts and zero-tolerance policies have been so successful? Or, could it be instead that the contagion effect has run its course?

> *Educators must learn to respond to a violent episode without . . . calling so much direct attention to it.*

It is perhaps a silver lining to America's concern in recent years over international terrorism—from Al Qaeda to anthrax—as well as about the war in Iraq. Such concerns have shifted attention away from school violence, thus allowing teachers to teach and students to learn without constantly fixating on school shootings and reinforcing the contagion.

At the same time, today's calm is a fragile one. Should some angry 14-year-old in Smalltown High decide to "do a Columbine," the hysteria would quickly resurface as would the threat of copycat behavior—that is, of course, unless we respond with good sense and reason.

9

Arming Teachers and Parents Will Prevent School Shootings

Doug Hagin

Doug Hagin is a conservative syndicated columnist.

School shootings are evil acts committed by monsters. It is futile to try to understand school shooters or to identify the causes of their behavior. Claims that violent video games, television shows, or the availability of guns cause such crimes are unwarranted. In fact, statistics show that in states that have right-to-carry concealed gun laws, violent crime decreases. Arming teachers and parents, not stronger gun control laws, will prevent future school shootings.

The tragic school shooting in Red Lake, Minnesota, has brought back some horrific memories from earlier times. Names of small towns like Columbine, Pearl, and Jonesboro[1] are all etched in our minds because of the evil acts committed there and the lives of innocent children, which were lost in those school shootings.

Now we are faced with coping with another senseless and barbaric act, and with more innocent lives lost at the hands of

---

1. At Columbine High School, in Littleton, Colorado, 12 students and one teacher were killed by Eric Harris and Dylan Klebold. At Pearl High School in Mississippi, Luke Woodham killed 2 students and wounded 7 others. At Westside Middle School in Jonesboro, Arkansas, two boys ages 11 and 13, killed 5 people and wounded 11 others.

an evil and twisted teen-age monster. Yes, monster is the only proper way to describe the individual who committed this heinous act.

Anyone who wants to feel empathy for this evil person or the evil acts he committed can just spare me their rhetoric. Spare me the well intended but useless calls to understand why he shot and killed those students and teachers. Spare me the babbling about the need for us to recognize why this person killed his grandfather, stole his guns, car, and bulletproof vest and then went on a killing spree.

Trying to Understand Makes No Sense

Sane, rational, caring human beings are frankly not able to understand such barbarism. We do not grasp such depraved behavior because people with normally functioning minds cannot possibly grasp such deeds. We can all talk . . . until our ears fall off about the need to understand serial killers and mass murderers and it will get us nowhere. Trying to understand such barbarity makes as much sense as putting a screen door in a submarine.

We will do ourselves no good by attempting to place the blame for [the Red Lake, Minnesota, school shooting] massacre anywhere except on the killer who carried it out.

Spare me as well these claims that our teachers should somehow possess some psychic abilities, which allow them to be able to see into the future and predict which troubled kids are capable of such murderous acts. Are we supposed to jerk every student who acts a little off out of class and force psychological screenings upon them? Sure, it would be nice if we could see the future and stop these acts, but in the real world, that is just a fantasy.

Likewise, we will do ourselves no good by attempting to place the blame for this massacre anywhere except on the killer who carried it out. Yet predictably, the same people have already started giving the same lame answers when asked what happened in Red Lake, Minnesota.

Violent Media Are Not Responsible

The same folks who somehow think video games are to blame are all too ready to take some of the responsibility off the shoulders of the killer and place it on violent video games instead. Yes, it is true there are some very violent and graphic games out there. Should parents think twice or more before buying them or allowing their kids to? Absolutely! However, when one considers that hundreds of thousands of people play these games regularly and never so much as harm a fly, the illogic of blaming school shootings on them falls on its face.

The same can be said of the folks eager to blame television or movies for this act. Maybe it eases our pain to think maybe violent broadcasts can twist a normal human mind to the point that it snaps, causing the person to go on a shooting spree. It might ease someone's mind but it will do nothing to stop future mass murders will it? After all murder predates TV or video games doesn't it?

Guns Are Not to Blame

Spare me most of all the moronic ranting and raving of the gun grabbers who always seem a little pleased when such tragedies happen and afford them an opportunity to blame guns and gun owners. Of all those who seek to deflect blame from the killer the gun control zealots are, by far, the most disturbing.

They spout the same tired lies about how the easy accessibility of guns is to blame, or America's love of guns and violence is at fault. No, no, and no again! The killer is at fault alone here. After all, he killed his grandfather and then took his guns. If you are willing to commit murder to get hold of a gun what law would stop you?

The facts are crystal clear on guns and violent crime. These acts are never committed where they know people are armed are they? In those states that allow citizens to carry concealed weapons violent crime decreases, doesn't it? Several of the school shootings in recent years have been stopped by law-abiding citizens with concealed carry permits, haven't they? There would have been more dead students if it were not for those law-abiding Americans and their firearms!

How do we prevent future school shootings?... First, allow teachers to carry guns if they have concealed carry permits. Secondly, allow any parents to carry and patrol the halls as well.

Yet the gun grabbers are still trying their level best to rescind concealed carry laws. They are still fabricating stats about how many children die by gunfire. They are still doing everything they can to disarm innocent people, thereby actually giving aid to criminals. Rest assured there was one thing this killer in Red Lake knew. He knew he would not face an armed teacher or principal while he slaughtered innocents. In addition, he had useless gun control laws and Liberals to thank for the fact his victims were helpless.

More gun control laws will not only not prevent future mass murders they will, in fact, only assure more of them will happen. Evil doers delight when no one is willing to face up to them, and gun grabbers certainly are not willing for anyone to stand up to evil doers. They seemingly prefer dead unarmed victims to citizens capable of defending themselves.

Teachers and Parents Should Be Armed

So how do we prevent future school shootings? Well we could use common sense in place of knee-jerk reactions. First, allow teachers to carry guns if they have concealed carry permits. Secondly, allow any parents to carry and patrol the halls as well. No one will have anything to fear from this, except anyone who would have evil intentions, that is.

Next we stop teaching our kids that they have no right to protect themselves or others. Evil thrives where no one stands against it, and too many schools teach that self-defense is somehow wrong. This only abets those with evil intentions. Defending ourselves is our right and duty, to teach anything else is delusional and wrong.

Sure, these might seem extreme steps to take. However, consider this question. Has evil ever been stopped by cowering before it or appeasing it?

10

Designing Safer Guns Will Reduce School Schootings

Ronald Brownstein

Ronald Brownstein has been a correspondent for the Los Angeles Times *since 1989.*

School shooters often use guns stolen from adults. One way to prevent future school shootings might therefore be to design a gun that can only be fired by its owner. Researchers have developed a prototype and are working to convince consumers that it will be reliable. In addition to other efforts to prevent school shootings, the U.S. government should encourage gun manufacturers to develop these guns as soon as possible.

It's still true, as Leo Tolstoy wrote long ago, that every unhappy family is unique in its misery. But in our time, the bridge between private despair and public tragedy, especially for young people, is often the same: stolen guns.

So it was in [the 2005] school massacre in Red Lake, Minn. No one can definitively say what created Jeff Weise's desire to kill. It may have had its roots in a shattered family, or an adverse reaction to antidepressant drugs, or simply humanity's innate capacity for evil. But there's less mystery about the factor that created his ability to kill 10 people, including himself, at his high school: When Weise shot his grandfather, a police officer, with a .22-caliber handgun and stole his shotgun and revolver, the young man's rage became much more dangerous to those around him.

Using Stolen Guns

In that way, the 16-year-old was hardly unique. Experts say that young people who commit school shootings often use guns stolen from adults; it could hardly be otherwise.

That pattern has drawn almost no attention in the killings' aftermath. The White House, the political establishment and even the media have treated the Minnesota shootings . . . as an inexplicable tragedy that underscores the persistence of school violence. But it ought to inspire us to ask what we can do to make such tragedies less frequent and, when they occur, less deadly.

The answer has many pieces, from improvements in school security to more effective counseling for troubled youths. But part of it could be no more complicated than making it tougher for young people to use guns that don't belong to them. In an era of personalized technology, it seems reasonable to ask why it isn't possible to design guns that can't be fired by anyone except their authorized user.

Technology Might Provide a Solution

That's the question being explored by researchers at the New Jersey Institute of Technology in Newark. In 2002, the New Jersey Legislature passed a groundbreaking measure encouraging the development of so-called smart guns that would not fire for anyone except their authorized owner.

No such guns exist today. But the New Jersey statute said the state would permit the sale of only "smart guns" three years after any manufacturer brought to the market a viable model.

The New Jersey Institute of Technology has been working to develop such a firearm since 1999, the last few years with the help of federal funds secured by its two Democratic senators, Jon Corzine and Frank R. Lautenberg. The institute, part of the state university system, spent the first few years examining alternative approaches for personalizing a gun to prevent anyone but its owner from firing it.

For the last several years, the institute has focused on "dynamic grip recognition" technology. That's a system enabling sensors in a gun's handle to recognize the owner's grip and then block anyone else from firing it.

"Smart Guns" Could Prevent Future Tragedies

"The basic concept is this—the way you grab the gun during the first incidence of the trigger pull becomes a coordinated and reflexive act," said Donald H. Sebastian, the institute's vice president for research and technology. "The fingerprint equivalent is the pressure pattern of your hand on the grip of the gun over time. We can see enough uniqueness in roughly the first tenth of a second of the trigger pull in order to be able to identify you as you."

The research has progressed enough that the institute demonstrated a prototype at a shooting range in Bayonne [New Jersey] [in December 2004]. But Sebastian estimates the effort is three years away from producing an actual gun that consumers will consider reliable enough to purchase.

Experts say that young people who commit school shootings often use guns stolen from adults.

The technical challenges are formidable. Before it could be sold, the institute's smart gun would need to demonstrate that it could recognize its owner if he was wearing gloves, or grabbed the gun in an unusual way under stress, or even picked it up with the hand other than the one he normally uses. Since many people buy guns for personal protection, the margin for error is understandably low.

Yet Sebastian is confident, based on the research so far, that these technical problems can be overcome. And, indeed, smart guns fit with the steady development of technology personalizing products for their users.

The Public Will Welcome Safer Guns

"When the public becomes more familiar with personalization technology, such as computers, it will come to understand that the technology is feasible and ought to be applied to guns as well," said Stephen Teret, a professor at the Johns Hopkins Bloomberg School of Public Health in Baltimore.

Washington could accelerate that process if it focused more on the potential. After the shootings at Colorado's Columbine High School in 1999, President [Bill] Clinton negotiated an agreement with Smith & Wesson in which the venerable gun maker agreed to develop smart guns, as well as to take other positive steps, such as installing locks on all guns.

But the company was battered by a boycott organized by gun-owner groups, which considered the deal a sellout of "gun rights." After a change of ownership, Smith & Wesson cooled on the agreement, and President [George W.] Bush allowed the company to back out of it. Today that once-promising effort is a dead letter.

One of a president's greatest tools is the power to enlarge—or diminish—the parameters of the possible. Bush said nothing in public about the Minnesota shootings for days, and when he finally mentioned it, in his radio address . . . , he alluded only to the need for more character education.

That's a worthwhile initiative. But the country deserves a more comprehensive approach to discouraging youth violence. Part of the answer could be expanded federal efforts to support the work in New Jersey and to spur gun manufacturers to explore other possibilities to prevent young people from killing with guns that don't belong to them. That's not left or right. It's just smart.

11

Gun Control Laws Will Not Stop School Shootings

Steve Chapman

Steve Chapman is a columnist and editorial writer for the Chicago Tribune. *He has also written for the* New Republic, Slate, American Spectator, Weekly Standard, Reason, *and* National Review.

Fewer people currently believe that tighter gun control laws will address the root causes of school violence. In the past most school shooting incidents have been followed by calls for stronger gun control legislation. However, advocates for gun control have been much less vocal in the aftermath of recent school shootings. Many now understand that school shootings are extremely rare and that strict gun control laws do not prevent school shooters from obtaining guns.

What is conspicuous about the aftermath of the school shootings in Red Lake, Minn., [in March 2005] was what didn't occur—a torrent of calls for new gun-control legislation.

The attack was the worst at a school since Columbine [in 1999]. It came on the heels of some other publicized eruptions of gun violence—including a rampage by a defendant at an Atlanta courthouse and a mass shooting at a worship service in a Milwaukee suburb. In the past, any of these might have spurred gun-control advocates into a major push for action. But this time, not much has happened, and not much is likely to.

Opinions About Gun Violence Have Changed

Why not? One simple reason is that Congress and the White House are both in the hands of Republicans, who generally aren't eager to impose restrictions on firearms. But maybe the Republicans are in power partly because of the new mood that has settled over the issue of gun violence.

Even the staunchest anti-gun organizations made only perfunctory efforts to capitalize on the Minnesota [school] shootings.

It has become clear over the years that most of these spectacular episodes are so freakish that they are not amenable to regulatory solutions. It has also become clear that any imaginable gun-control laws are not likely to have much effect on crime in America.

Even the staunchest anti-gun organizations made only perfunctory efforts to capitalize on the Minnesota shootings. The Brady Campaign to Prevent Gun Violence used the opportunity to criticize Congress for letting the federal "assault weapons" ban expire, mandating immediate destruction of the records of gun sales, and considering a bill to limit lawsuits against gun dealers.

Laws Can Not Stop Gun Theft

But these had nothing to do with what happened in Red Lake. Records of gun sales? The killer, Jeff Weise, 16, wasn't old enough to buy a gun legally in Minnesota. At least two of his

73

guns were stolen from his grandfather, a police officer whom he killed.

Assault weapons ban? His arsenal included no such weapons—only a .22-caliber pistol, plus a police-issued .40-caliber handgun and 12-gauge shotgun. Limiting lawsuits against dealers? A bill that hasn't been enacted couldn't have caused a mass shooting yet.

A Love Affair with Guns?

The Violence Policy Center charged that the problem lies in "America's love affair with guns," and held up the example of countries that, it says, have prevented mass shootings through "severe restrictions on the availability of specific classes of firearms, such as handguns and assault weapons." This statement only confirmed the National Rifle Association's suspicion that gun-control advocates are bent on banning entire categories of common firearms—even though most owners use them in a responsible and law-abiding manner.

But decrying America's love affair with guns is like decrying America's love affair with football or movies. There are some 260 million firearms in private hands in this country. Any solution requiring vast numbers of people to reject something they have long valued is not a solution but a fantasy. It's also an admission that no politically feasible options are likely to have any perceptible effect on crime.

Gun-control advocates have been losing ground with the public. In 1990, 78 percent of Americans said they thought laws on firearm sales should be stricter. By 2004, only 54 percent agreed. By a 2-1 margin, they oppose a general ban on private ownership of handguns—as dreamed of by the Violence Policy Center. When Congress let the "assault weapons" ban expire [in 2004] there was no public uproar.

Schools Are Actually Safer Now

Past experience with school shootings, horrific as they are, may have also made people skeptical of overreaction. As it happens, this sort of mayhem is rare and getting rarer. [A 2004] federal report on school crime and safety notes that the number of kids killed at school dropped from 33 in the 1998–99 school year to 14 in 2001–02. Other violent crimes against students at school have also declined.

[Gun-control laws that require] vast numbers of people to reject something that they have long valued is not a solution [to school shootings] but a fantasy.

Common-sense security measures, like limiting access to schools by outsiders, may help. But eliminating such shootings entirely is asking too much. Says Ronald Stephens, executive director of the California-based National School Safety Center, "It's very difficult to stop an incident like this unless you have an army standing at the door."

Most Americans have probably figured that out, and while they may be shocked and saddened by mass murder, they don't expect it to ever be eradicated. That sort of realism is no ally of gun control.

12

School Testing Programs Overshadow School Shooting Prevention Programs

Margaret McKenna and David Haselkorn

Margaret McKenna, president of Lesley University in Cambridge, Massachusetts, served as White House deputy counsel to President Jimmy Carter, and as deputy under secretary at the U.S. Department of Education. David Haselkorn is dean of National Education Programs and Policy at Lesley University.

The 1999 school shooting at Columbine High School, in Littleton, Colorado, focused attention on the need to create supportive, nurturing communities in school settings. However, the No Child Left Behind Act forces teachers and school administrators to focus on achieving yearly improvement on standardized tests. The result of this intensive emphasis on testing is that the most important lesson of the school shootings, the need for a personalized and responsive school environment that supports the development of emotionally healthy children, has been eclipsed.

[In 1999], automatic weapons fire echoed through the halls of Columbine High School in Littleton, Colo., shattering lives, complacency, and the idea of suburban schools as safe havens. The attack focused national attention on issues of

Margaret McKenna and David Haselkorn, "No Child Left Behind and the Lessons of Columbine," *USA Today,* May 2005. Copyright © 2005 by the Society for the Advancement of Education. Reproduced by permission.

safety, student isolation, bullying, and the victimization that depersonalized school environments seem to foster. There was widespread acknowledgment that teachers and administrators needed to find ways to get to know kids better and create real communities in our learning institutions.

It was a deadly reminder that education not only is about teaching content, but supporting and developing human beings. The lessons of Columbine have brought beefed up security and attention to school safety. Metal detector sales have flourished. New school crisis response plans and security measures are in place. Halls are under more surveillance. Community law enforcement agencies are cooperating more closely with school officials, and schools, out of necessity, are being run in a more regimented way. Teachers and administrators now at least know where their students are, if not who they are.

Real Learning Has Not Occurred

Yet, it appears that many of the most important lessons of Columbine have been set aside. The No Child Left Behind Act's [NCLB's] unrelenting focus on yearly improvement in test scores has forced many schools to narrow their goals for students in ways that comply with the law's intent. There are, however, unintended consequences. The resulting impact on school climate, in particular, raises concern. As class time becomes more regimented and tight budgets create larger classes, schools are becoming environments even less conducive for teachers to know their students well. NCLB forces communities to focus more on raising test scores than on raising kids.

While it is true that statistics on school violence show a decline since 1995, incidents of bullying and victimization are on the upswing. An American Medical Association report estimates that more than 3,200,000 students in grades six through 10 are victims of moderate or serious bullying each year. In its report on the causes of school violence after Columbine, the

Secret Service indicated that nearly three-fourths of perpetrators of deadly school violence reported a history of having been bullied.

[The shooting at Columbine High School] . . . was a deadly reminder that education not only is about teaching content, but supporting and developing human beings.

A growing number of states are instituting laws to combat bullying, and there even is money in NCLB that districts can use to fund such programs. However, piecemeal responses are not going to have much effect, especially in the wake of NCLB's overwhelming focus on student achievement, narrowly defined as Adequate Yearly Progress on annual standardized tests. Raising student achievement is important, but history has taught some hard lessons concerning what happens when a single-minded focus on test scores replaces a more comprehensive set of indicators for what constitutes a successful school.

Across the country, schools are reporting that the pressures of NCLB-mandated testing regimes are crowding out teacher time and forcing cutbacks in such "frills" as art, music, phys-ed, and recess, all of which are not perceived to translate into immediate bottom line success in raising test scores. In a survey of elementary school principals, 25% report decreased instructional time for the arts, and 33% anticipate future cuts. An estimated 40% of elementary schools have reduced or eliminated recess. In their place are more test prep and drills, as well as reports of increasing levels of regimentation, student alienation, and teacher stress. More worrisome still is the growing belief that rising test scores alone equate to successful schools.

The Test Score Dilemma

The test scores at Columbine High School were among the

highest in Colorado. Tragedy, however, still ensued, just as it did in Cowers, Ga.; Santana, Calif.; and, . . . in Redlake, Minn. Teachers and administrators may fail to see the warning signs because of the focus on the measures of school performance that can be counted (like test scores), not the ones that most likely deter these tragedies.

Teachers and administrators may fail to see the warning signs because of the focus on the measures of school performance that can be counted . . . not the ones that most likely deter [school shootings].

Creativity, problem-solving skills, respect for differences, excitement about learning, self-esteem, civic engagement, and school climate are barometers of school and student success for which test scores are, at best, a weak proxy. Performing well on math and literacy tests is not the sole predictor of performing well as members of society. Yet, the reality that a number of schools have been labeled "underperforming" by NCLB standards raises the stakes even higher. Teachers will be pressured to concentrate still greater efforts on drill and test rather than on developing broadly educated students and, more importantly, responsible and engaged future citizens. . . .

A More Balanced Approach Is Needed

Higher standards and better measures of student achievement are a good thing, although they are by no means the entire package—and absent a much stronger focus on other dimensions of learning and development, they will lead to predictably perverse outcomes within our educational system and in the lives of schoolchildren. . . .

Strip away the ideological turf wars that inflect our educational discourse and you often arrive at fundamentally opposite views of learning, human nature, and the role of education in a democracy. NCLB is influenced deeply by the market-based philosophies of its prime, neoconservative movers. Markets inherently create winners and losers. The rhetoric of leaving no child behind is belied by a system geared to a narrow standardization of goals that results in a diminished realm of opportunity to demonstrate accomplishment and achievement.

The development of a free, informed, productive, and engaged future citizenry depends on our ability to develop healthy children first.

The result is an increasingly rigged system that favors the affluent child whose parents have the wherewithal to make up what we systematically are taking away from our public schools in the drive to promote standards-based instruction and adequate yearly progress. Consider the endless array of enrichment experiences the well-to-do are able to purchase in the free market: soccer camps, SAT/test prep, community theater classes, summer programs for the arts, college application consultants, learning-style coaches, homework helpers, music lessons—the list goes on and on. It is a good list. Children should have all types of opportunities to develop their interests, talents, imaginations, intellect, and character. But this should be accomplished at school (or neighborhood centers associated with them), in classrooms that have authentic connections to the community, and through teachers who are competent, caring, qualified, well-paid, and supported, backed up by systems that are organized to promote student success and development because they are informed by a real understanding of child and adolescent development, community context, the value of diversity, the importance of play, the centrality of civic engagement, and (of course) the mastery of challenging academic content.

Our present approach to school reform confuses a question of means (what students know and are able to do) with one of ends (who students are and can hope to become). In so doing, it fails to take public education's crucial role in our pluralistic democracy seriously enough. The development of a free, informed, productive, and engaged future citizenry depends on our ability to develop healthy children first.

13

Victims of School Shootings Struggle to Rebuild Their Lives

Vickie Bane and Jason Bane

Vickie Bane and Jason Bane are writers for People *magazine.*

Years after Dylan Klebold and Eric Harris murdered thirteen people and wounded twenty-three at Columbine High School, in Littleton, Colorado, their victims and their families wrestle with painful memories, disability, and loss. In the following selection some of the victims of the Columbine shooting talk about what happened that fateful day, their attitudes toward the shooters then and now, and how they have learned to cope.

Sean Graves

One of the first students shot, he taught himself to walk again with grit and the support of people around the world.

Walking with Hard Work. For three years he had been waiting for this moment. Sitting nervously in his wheelchair at the May 2002 graduation ceremony of his class at Columbine High, Sean Graves heard his name called. With hardly a wobble, he arose from his wheelchair and walked to the podium for his diploma—as his classmates and hundreds of spectators came to their feet in a roaring ovation. It was the first time he had walked in public since the day the 15-year-old freshman was hit by a bullet fired by Eric Harris that grazed his spine and partially paralyzed him. "I wanted to make sure these people knew I didn't do it for myself," says Graves. "I did it to show that things are possible with prayer and hard work."

Why would I spend so much time and energy hating two people who aren't even in this world anymore? . . . I just focused all my attention on recovering.

Graves acknowledges that in the aftermath of the tragedy he "despised" the killers. But slowly he started to realize that the road to a more normal life would start with letting go. "Why should I spend so much time and energy hating two people who aren't even in this world anymore." he says. "I just focused all my attention on recovering," He has undergone eight surgical procedures and spent hundreds of hours in physical therapy.

He still uses a cane to get around, but plans to finish up soon at Red Rocks Community College and get a job rebuilding computers. Even now Graves talks often about how grateful he is for the support he received from people around the world, as evidenced by the eight duffel bags of mail he has in his basement. One message he especially treasures is a note he received from Christopher Reeve, whom he met at two spinal-research fund-raisers the actor hosted in Vail [Colorado] and whose courage helped give him strength. Wrote Reeve of hearing about Graves's steps on the stage: "I was your inspiration, and now you are mine."

Kacey Ruegsegger

Years after coming face-to-face with the killers, she could not shake a sense of dread.

The Wounds Were Emotional as Well as Physical. "I knew who shot me," says Kacey Ruegsegger of the moment when Harris confronted her in the school library, as she huddled fearfully under a table. "I remember looking straight down the barrel." In the next instant the shotgun blast blew a hole in her right shoulder and her hand. "I made a moaning noise, I guess," recalls Ruegsegger. "The gunman told me, 'Quit your bitching.' I thought he was going to shoot me again, so I pretended to be dead." Adds Ruegsegger: "I was the only one out of the first six shot in the library who survived."

The physical injuries she suffered that day were bad enough, but the lasting psychological scars have proved just as debilitating. "I used to have panic attacks all the time, the first three or four years," says Ruegsegger, 22. "If somebody walked into a restaurant with a suspicious bag, I would be gone." There were times when she had difficulty calming herself. "I'd be shaking and have this overwhelming sense of doom," she says. "It was like somebody else just comes inside me and takes over—it was the worst feeling." Until recently she could not bring herself to enter any library, for any reason, even after she enrolled at Colorado State University.

I used to have panic attacks all the time, the first three or four years.... If somebody walked into a restaurant with a suspicious bag, I would be gone.

In 2001 she had an epiphany—she wanted to be a nurse. As her mother, Darcy, explains, it is a way for Kacey to "give back" for having her own life spared. There has been other progress as well. In February she steeled herself and went into a library for the first time. "I called my mom," says Kacey, who expects to finish her nursing studies at Arapahoe Community College this December [2004]. "I was so excited." But she doesn't fool herself into thinking that the shadow over her has been entirely lifted. "I have my faith, and I look like I'm doing great," she says. "But there are days, I'm sure for all of us, that it's not okay."

The Mauser Family

In memory of their son, a crusade for gun control; at home, a new child brings joy and hope.

Activism Helps the Healing Process. "You don't get over it," says Tom Mauser, whose 15-year-old son Daniel was killed in the library at Columbine. "But you have to be honest with yourself that your child would not want you to be in deep grief and anger for the rest of your life." And yet those two emotions have continued to influence his life in profound ways. Almost from the first days after the tragedy, Mauser, 52, emerged as a passionate advocate of stricter gun-control measures, visiting the White House and lobbying the state legislature. His efforts paid off in November 2000, when Colorado voted to become, along with Oregon, one of the first states in the country to close the so-called gun-show loophole, which had allowed the purchase of firearms at such events without background checks.

> *You have to be honest with yourself that your child would not want you to be in deep grief and anger for the rest of your life.*

Mauser received much credit for getting the initiative passed—but he also became the target of death threats from opponents. Meanwhile wife Linda, 52, began urging that the couple, who also have a daughter, Christine, 18, adopt a baby. In October 2000 they picked up their new daughter, Madeline, now 4, in China. "We recognized that she was not a replacement for Daniel," says Tom, "but still we had room for her in our hearts." And indeed the newest member of the family has proved a true blessing. "She's amazing," says Tom. "She's given me something to look forward to." Tom doesn't speak as much in public these days, but when he does, he always stumbles over the part where he tells the audience, "My son died." Says Tom, his eyes filling with tears: "Those words are still hard to say."

Richard Castaldo

A movie role, a band and a budding business help ease what has been a difficult path.

Things Take More Time. He can sound remarkably matter-of-fact. "There's not too much that bothers me now physically, it just takes a lot longer to do stuff," says Richard Castaldo, 22, who suffered a bullet wound to the spine that left him in a wheelchair. "I'm about as adjusted to it as I'm going to get." And in some ways that is quite well adjusted indeed. Passionate about music, he plays bass guitar in a rock band, Danger Girl. With money from a fund set up in his name, he was able to purchase an apartment building in South Denver as well as a house for himself nearby. A featured role in Michael Moore's documentary *Bowling for Columbine* proved another plus. "It was cool, because after that it was more like 'Hey, you're from that movie,' rather than 'You're from the school-shooting thing,'" he says.

It upsets him that he wasn't doing anything. He was just eating lunch, and now his whole life has changed.

But Castaldo also feels a private anguish. "I think the anger has started to seep into Richard," says his mother, Connie Birdsell-Michalik, 48. "It upsets him that he wasn't doing anything. He was just eating lunch, and now his whole life has changed." Still, the one thing Richard insists he doesn't allow himself to do anymore is wonder, "What if?" "I used to a little bit, but then I realized it's just stupid," he says. "You'll drive yourself insane trying to think about that."

Anne Marie Hochhalter

On an 'evil' day that left her with grievous wounds, she was saved by a couple of timely miracles.

"A Lot of Things Went So Right." Anne Marie Hochhalter had just gone outside to soak up some of the warm midday sun when she heard a popping noise behind her. Then something struck her in the back. It hurt, but she thought it was from a paintball gun. As a friend helped her, another bullet hit, this time tearing a critical vein. "I was bleeding to death," recalls Hochhalter, 22. "It didn't look bad on the outside, but inside it felt wrong—it felt wet."

A lot of evil happened that day, . . . but a lot of things went so right.

The way Hochhalter sees it, even though the attack left her paralyzed and wheelchair bound, she was nonetheless quite lucky. "If the ambulance had come two minutes later—even two minutes—I would have died," says Hochhalter. Her good fortune continued when she got to the hospital, where surgeons, prepped to start operating on a heart patient, took her instead. "A lot of evil happened that day," says Hochhalter, "but a lot of things went so right."

In the months after, though, it was a different story. Her mother, Carla, soon started showing serious signs of bipolar disorder. In October [2003] she committed suicide. "I don't think she knew what she was doing," says Hochhalter. "Which is kind of like Eric and Dylan—I don't think they knew what they were doing." Now living in her own townhouse and taking business courses at the University of Colorado–Denver

Center, Hochhalter draws comfort from her involvement in a local church and a close relationship she has developed with Sue Townsend, 55, whose stepdaughter Lauren, 18, was one of those killed at Columbine. "When I look at Anne Marie," says Townsend, "I feel Lauren smiling on me."

Patrick Ireland

Once known as the tragic 'boy in the window,' he now looks ahead to a bright future.

Living His Life. He remembers when the shooters came into the library. "They said, 'Everybody with white hats [which were customarily worn by many of the school's athletes], stand up. This is for all the s—— you've put us through for the past four years.'" Then the carnage started. Pat Ireland, now 22, was shot three times, including twice in the head, which knocked him out for roughly three hours. Somehow, despite being paralyzed on his entire right side, when he came to, he was able to crawl 50 feet to the window. A photo of him desperately plunging through the shattered glass of the second-story library onto the roof of a waiting rescue vehicle became one of the most indelible images of the tragedy.

Five years later one of the bullets is still lodged in Ireland's head, but memories of the horror seem amazingly far from his mind. "You can think about it and dwell on it for a limited amount of time," says Ireland, who spent months in rehab after the attack and still has trouble gripping with his right hand and walks with a slight limp. "But then you've just got to kind of accept it and start living your life the best you can." Toward that end he has earned a 3.9 GPA as a finance major at Colorado State University, is looking forward to entering graduate school and has a girlfriend, Kacie Lancaster, who is an aspiring model. And he often goes back to visit Columbine High. "I love that school," he says. "It's my school."

For the Killers' Parents, Unending Questions

In the immediate aftermath of the shootings, Dylan Klebold's parents, Tom and Sue, fled their comfortable home in Deer Creek Canyon to seek privacy in their grief. Already, though, a sign reading "Sue & Tom We [love] You. We're Here for You. Call Us" and bearing the signatures of many of their neighbors had been placed on one of their fences. The couple soon returned home but didn't seem inclined to reach out to many of those who offered them support. "My sense is they've kind of withdrawn from social contact," says one neighbor, who has occasionally seen them walking on nearby trails.

Tom, 57, still operates his mortgage-and-property company from a home office, and Sue, 55, has kept her position as a college job-placement official for the disabled, where she has earned the respect of many coworkers. "I have never seen anybody as strong," says one colleague. "She read every letter that she received—supportive and nonsupportive. She has tried to understand what happened head-on." In much the same way, Eric Harris's parents, Wayne and Kathy, have also stayed in the Columbine area. Wayne, 55, continues to work developing pilot-training programs, and Kathy, 54, a caterer, recently helped plan her son Kevin's wedding. They, too, have a very tight circle of friends. "They are getting back to some semblance of a normal life, and I'm putting quotes around normal," says longtime friend Carl Payne, who lives in Plattsburgh, N.Y. "What they've gone through I would call a nightmare." And most painful, it is a nightmare foretold by the two killers, who made a three-hour tape before their rampage that practically boasted of what lay in store for the parents they professed to love. "They're going to go through hell once we're finished," said Eric Harris on the tape. "They're never going to see the end of it."

Organizations to Contact

American Academy of Child and
Adolescent Psychiatry (AACAP)
3615 Wisconsin Ave. NW
  Washington, DC 20016-3007
(202) 966-7300 • fax: (202) 966-2891
Web site: www.aacap.org

AACAP is the leading national professional medical association committed to treating the 7 to 12 million American youth suffering from mental, behavioral, and developmental disorders. It publishes the monthly *Journal of the American Academy of Child and Adolescent Psychiatry* and the fact sheets "Children and TV Violence," "Understanding Violent Behavior in Children and Adolescents," and "Children's Threats: When Are They Serious?"

American Academy of Pediatrics (AAP)
141 Northwest Point Blvd.
  Elk Grove Village, IL 60007
(847) 434-4000 • fax: (847) 434-8000
Web site: www.aap.org

The American Academy of Pediatrics is an association of more than sixty thousand physicians who are committed to the attainment of optimal physical, mental, and well-being of infants, children, adolescents, and young adults. The AAP publishes the monthly journal, *Pediatrics*. Position papers on school violence, gun control, and the impact of the media on violent behavior, including "The Jonesboro School Shootings: Lessons for Us All," are available on its Web site.

American Civil Liberties Union (ACLU)
125 Broad St., 18th Fl.
  New York, NY 10004

(212) 549-2585 • fax: (212) 549-2646
Web site: www.aclu.org

The ACLU is a national organization that works to defend Americans' civil rights as guaranteed by the U.S. Constitution. It works to establish equality before the law, regardless of race, color, sexual orientation, or national origin. The ACLU publishes and distributes the semiannual newsletter *Civil Liberties Alert,* policy statements, pamphlets, reports, including "Making Schools Safe," which is available on its Web site.

Center for the Prevention of School Violence
1801 Mail Service Center
   Raleigh, NC 27699-1801
(919) 733-3388 • fax: (800) 299-6054
e-mail: nadine.lewis@ncmail.net
Web site: www.ncdjjdp.org/cpsv

The Center for the Prevention of School Violence is a clearinghouse for information, programs, and research about school violence and its prevention. The center also provides information about all aspects of the problems that fall under the heading of school violence as well as information about strategies that are directed at solving these problems.

National Alliance for Safe Schools
PO Box 290, Slanesville, WV 25445
(888) 510-6500 • fax: (304) 496-8105
e-mail: nass@raven-villages.net
Web site: www.safeschools.org

Founded in 1977 by a group of school security directors, the National Alliance for Safe Schools was established to provide training, security assessments, and technical assistance to school districts interested in reducing school-based crime and violence. It publishes the book *Making Schools Safe for Students.*

National Criminal Justice Reference Service (NCJRS)
PO Box 6000, Rockville, MD 20849-6000

(800) 851-3420
e-mail: askncjrs@ncjrs.org
Web site: www.ncjrs.org

A component of the Office of Justice Programs of the U.S. Department of Justice, the NCJRS supports research on crime, criminal behavior, and crime prevention. The National Criminal Justice Reference Service acts as a clearinghouse for criminal justice information for researchers and other interested individuals. Among the numerous reports it publishes and distributes are "Addressing Bullying in Schools: Theory and Practice," "Crime in the Schools: Reducing Conflict with Student Problem Solving," and "Preventing School Shootings: A Summary of a U.S. Secret Service School Initiative Report."

The Oregon Social Learning Center (OSLC)
160 E. Fourth Ave., Eugene, OR 97401
(541) 485-2711 • fax: (541) 485-7087
Web site: www.oslc.org

OSLC is a nonprofit, independent research center dedicated to finding ways to help children and parents as they cope with daily problems. The center is known for its successful work in designing and implementing interventions for children and parents to help encourage successful adjustment and discourage aggressive behaviors within the family, the school, and the community. OSLC has published over four hundred articles in scientific journals, many of which are available in an online database.

**Partners Against Violence Network
(PAVNET) Online**
(301) 504-5462
e-mail: jgladsto@nalusda.gov
Web site: www.pavnet.org

PAVNET Online is a virtual library of information about violence and youth at risk, representing data from seven different federal agencies. Its programs promote the prevention of youth violence through education as well as through sports and recreation. Among PAVNET's curricula publications are *Creative Conflict Solving for Kids* and *Escalating Violence: The Impact of Peers.* The monthly *PAVNET Online* newsletter is also available at its Web site as are articles on school violence.

U.S. Department of Education

400 Maryland Ave. SW
  Washington, DC 20202
(800) USA-LEARN • fax: (202) 401-0689
e-mail: customerservice@inet.ed.gov
Web site: www.ed.gov

The Safe and Drug-Free Schools Program is the U.S. Department of Education's primary vehicle for reducing drug, alcohol, and tobacco use, and violence through education and prevention activities in America's schools. It publishes the reports *Threat Assessment in Schools: A Guide to Managing Threatening Situations and to Creating Safe School Climates* and *Student-Led Crime Prevention: A Real Resource with Powerful Promise.*

Youth Crime Watch of America

9300 S. Dadeland Blvd., Suite 100
  Miami, FL 33156
(305) 670-2409 • fax: (305) 670-3805
e-mail: ycwa@ycwa.org
Web site: www.ycwa.org

Youth Crime Watch of America is a nonprofit organization that assists youth in actively reducing crime and drug use in their schools and communities. Its resources include handbooks for adult advisers and youth on starting and operating a Youth Crime Watch program, a *Getting Started* video, a *Mentoring Activities* handbook, and a *Talking with Youth About Prevention* teaching guide.

Internet Sources

The Killer at Thurston High
Web site: www.pbs.org/wgbh/pages/
frontline/shows/kinkel

A PBS *Frontline* special tells the story of Kip Kinkel, who was fifteen years old when he opened fire on classmates in his Springfield, Oregon, school, killing two and wounding fifteen.

A Timeline of School Shootings
www.infoplease.com/ipa/A0777958.html

This Web page provides a time line of school shootings that have occurred since 1996.

Warning Signs of Youth Violence
www.apahelpcenter.org/featuredtopics/feature.php?id=38

A featured topic on the American Psychological Association (APA) Web site, this resource examines the reasons for school shootings and other forms of youth violence, including information on risk factors and warning signs.

Bibliography

Books

Brooks Brown and Rob Merritt	*No Easy Answers: The Truth Behind Death at Columbine.* New York: Lantern, 2002.
Loren Coleman	*The Copycat Effect: How Media and Popular Culture Trigger the Mayhem in Tomorrow's Headlines.* New York: Paraview Pocketbooks, 2004.
Barbara Coloroso	*The Bully, the Bullied, and the Bystander: From Preschool to High School—How Parents and Teachers Can Help Break the Cycle of Violence.* New York: HarperCollins, 2003.
Alexander DeConde	*Gun Violence in America: The Struggle for Control.* Boston: Northeastern University Press, 2001.
SuEllen Fried	*Bullies, Targets, and Witnesses: Helping Children Break the Pain Chain.* New York: M. Evans, 2003.
David Grossman	*Stop Teaching Our Kids to Kill: A Call to Action Against TV, Movie, and Video Game Violence.* New York: Crown, 1999.
Jane Katch	*Under Dead Man's Skin: Discovering the Meaning of Children's Violent Play.* Boston: Beacon, 2001.
Joseph T. McCann	*Threats in Schools: A Practical Guide for Managing Violence.* New York: Haworth, 2002.

Mark Harrison Moore — *Deadly Lessons: Understanding Lethal School Violence.* Washington, DC: National Academy Press, 2003.

National Center for Education Statistics — *Crime and Safety in America's Public Schools: Selected Findings from the School Survey on Crime and Safety.* Washington, DC: U.S. Department of Education, 2004.

Katherine S. Newman — *Rampage: The Social Roots of School Shootings.* New York: Basic Books, 2004.

Lionel Shriver — *We Need to Talk About Kevin.* New York: Counterpoint, 2003.

Robert J. Spitzer — *The Politics of Gun Control.* Washington, DC: CQ Press, 2004.

Todd Strasser — *Give a Boy a Gun.* New York: Simon & Schuster, 2000.

Julie A. Webber — *Failure to Hold: The Politics of School Violence.* Lanham, MD: Rowman & Littlefield, 2003.

Gabriel Wiemann — *Communicating Unreality: Modern Media and the Reconstruction of Reality.* Thousand Oaks, CA: Sage, 2000.

Wendy Murray Zoba — *Day of Reckoning: Columbine and the Search for America's Soul.* Grand Rapids, MI: Brazos, 2000.

Periodicals

AScribe Health News Service — "Professor: Stop Explaining 'Why' When Kids Kill: Instead, Reach Out," April 26, 2005.

AScribe Law News Service	"Preventing School Shootings May Require Rethinking Individual Liberties, Duke Legal Scholar Says," March 22, 2005.
Heron Marquez Estrada, Ron Nixon, and John Stefany	"Red Lake School Shootings: An Internet Trail of a Boy's Death Wish," *Minneapolis Star Tribune,* March 24, 2005.
Jonathan D. Fast	"After Columbine: How People Mourn Sudden Death," *Social Work,* October, 2003.
Michelle Hainer	"21st Teen: After One of Angelita Ali's Classmates Was Shot, She Decided to Do Something to End Violence in Schools," *Teen People,* April 1, 2005.
Investor's Business Daily	"Armed with the Truth," March 23, 2005.
Dirk Johnson	"A Bloody Day on the Rez: A Columbine Copycat Shatters the Calm in Minnesota," *Newsweek,* April 4, 2005.
Jaana Juvenon	"Myths and Facts About Bullying in Schools: Effective Interventions Depend upon Debunking Long-Held Misconceptions," *Behavioral Health Management,* March/April, 2005.
Jeff Kass	"A Tragedy Averted," *Rocky Mountain News,* April 16, 2005.
Jeff Kass and Angie C. Marek	"What Happened After Columbine," *U.S. News & World Report,* April 4, 2005.
Mike Kennedy	"Responding to Tragedy," *American School & University,* April 1, 2004.

Chris Magg	"The Devil in Red Lake: Jeff Weise Lost His Parents but Had Close Friends. So Why Did He Shoot and Kill His Granddad and Eight Others?" *Time*, April 4, 2005.
Tony Manolatos	"Tip Makes Idaho Girl a Hero," *Detroit News*, September 21, 2004.
Glenn Muschart	"Columbine Coverage Shook the Nation," *USA Today*, August 23, 2003.
Ted Olsen	"Columbine's Other Tragedy," *Christianity Today*, March 2003.
Peter Piazza	"Scourge of the Schoolyard: Technology Alone Isn't Enough," *Security Management*, November, 2001.
Thomas Schmoll	"Masculinity and School Shootings— Gender Public Advocacy Coalition Says Common Thread Is Overlooked in Media Coverage," *America's Intelligence Wire*, March 22, 2005.
Douglas C. Smith and Daya S. Sandhu	"Toward a Positive Perspective on Violence Prevention in Schools," *Journal of Counseling and Development*, Summer 2004.
John Temple	"It's Impossible to Ignore Pain of Columbine," *Rocky Mountain News*, February 28, 2004.
Suzanne Tochterman	"From Horror to Healing: How Columbine Impacted Student Perspectives," *Reclaiming Children and Youth*, Winter 2002.
USA Today	"Columbine Coverage Shook the Nation," August 2003.
Edyth Wheeler	"Confronting Social Exclusion and Bullying," *Childhood Education*, Fall 2004.

Index

abuse, 21, 39, 41, 43–45
  see also bullying
accidental deaths, 21
Adequate Yearly Progress, 78, 80
administrators, 39, 41–42, 60, 76–77, 79
adolescents. *See* teenagers, violence and
adults, 17, 34
alienation, 33, 56, 58, 60–61, 78
  see also marginalization
anger, 50–51, 60
antidepressant drugs, 46–54, 68
assaults, 21, 24
assault weapons, 73–74
athletes, 39–45, 88

Baadsgaard, Cory, 53–54
Bane, Jason, 82
Bane, Vickie, 82
behavior, antisocial, 34
  see also bullying; violence
Beltway snipers, 28, 30
Best, Joel, 18
Bishop Neumann High School, shootings at, 48–49
Bowling for Columbine (documentary), 86
boys, 8, 33, 55–58
Brownstein, Ronald, 68
Bull Run Middle School, shootings at, 29–30
bullying, 18–20, 23–27, 39–45, 56–61, 77–78
Bush, Elizabeth, 48
Bush, George W., 71

Carneal, Michael, 8, 11–12
Castaldo, Richard, 86–87
Celexa, 49
Chapman, Steve, 72

cities, 12–13, 15, 17, 23
Clabaugh, Alison A., 39
Clabaugh, Gary K., 39
Clinton, Bill, 71
clothing. *See* goth clothing; trench coats
Columbine High School, 39–45
  lessons of, 29, 58, 76–79, 82–90
  shootings at, 7, 11–12, 19–20, 23–24, 47, 49
commando video games, 30
community, lack of, 59, 61, 76
concealed weapon permits, 63, 66–67
Conyers, Georgia, shootings in, 11
copycatting, 15, 31, 62
counseling, 69
crime rates, 21–23, 32–33, 66, 75
culture, 7, 21, 23, 36

deaths, numbers of, 16–17, 20–22, 30, 75
Department of Defense (DOD), 29–31
discrimination, 13, 80
disrespect, climate of, 59, 61
DOOM (video game), 7
drug-related homicides, 15, 17
drugs, reactions to, 46–54, 68

Ecstasy, 48
Edinboro, Pennsylvania, shootings in, 11
education, role of, 76–81
Effexor, 49, 54
epidemic view, 11, 14–15, 20–23, 32–33
Erfurt (Germany), shootings in, 16
expression, forms of, 9, 36–38

fairy tales, 36
families, problems in, 33, 68
fear, 10, 14–15, 17, 39, 59–60, 62
fighting. *See* violence
films, 7, 56–57, 65
First Amendment, 7, 9, 36
first-person shooter video games,
  7–9
Fluvoxamine. *See* Luvox
Fox, James Alan, 59
Full Spectrum Warrior (video
  game), 28, 30

gang-related homicides, 15, 17
girls, 8, 33, 34–35, 55, 57
GlaxoSmithKline Inc., 51
Golden, Andrew, 11
goth clothing, 56
Granite Hills High School, shootings in, 12, 49
Graves, Sean, 82–83
gun-control laws, 23, 85
  are not effective, 63, 65–66,
    72–75
guns, 7–9, 56–57, 68–71
gun-show loophole, 85

Hagin, Doug, 63
Halo (video game), 28–30
harassment, sexual, 39, 41–43, 45
Harris, Eric, 11, 19, 40–42, 44–50,
  58, 82–84, 87, 90
Harris, Kathy and Wayne
  (parents), 89–90
Haselkorn, David, 76
hazing, 41, 43
Heath, Kentucky, 13
Hicks, Seth, 55
Hitler, Adolf, 40, 56, 58
Hochhalter, Anne Marie, 87–88
Hoffman, Jason, 12, 49
home life, quality of, 33, 68

homicides, 14–15, 17, 21, 50–52
  see also school shootings
hype view, 14–15
hypoglycemia, 52

Internet, the, 56
intimidation, 39, 45
  see also bullying
Ireland, Patrick, 88–89
isolation, 37, 77
  see also alienation

Jenkins, Henry, 32
Johnson, Mitchell, 11
Jonesboro, Arkansas, shootings in,
  7, 11, 20

killing simulation video games,
  28, 30–31
Kinkel, Kip, 11, 48
Klebold, Dylan, 11, 19, 40–42,
  44–45, 47, 50, 58, 82, 87
Klebold, Sue and Tom (parents),
  89

law enforcement, 27, 77
lawsuits, 46–47, 49–54, 73–74
Levin, Jack, 59
Littleton, Colorado, 23
  see also Columbine High
    School
loners. *See* outcasts
LSD, 48
Luvox, 46–52

Malvo, Lee Boyd, 28–29
mania, 48–49
marginalization, 19, 44–45
Mauser family, 85–86
McKenna, Margaret, 76
media

coverage of shootings by, 10, 13–15, 17–27, 56–57
violence in, 7–9, 33–34, 38, 65
mental stability, 33
metal detectors, 27, 60, 77
Metal Gear Solid 2 (video game), 28, 30
military-style video games, 7–9, 28, 30–31, 35–36
Mortal Kombat (video game), 7
movies, 7, 56–57, 65
Muhammad, John Allen, 28
murders. *See* homicides

National Crime Victimization Survey, 22
neo-Nazism, 56
Newman, Katherine S., 10
newspapers, 14
No Child Left Behind Act (NCLB), 76–80

Olson, Christine, 11–12
O'Meara, Kelly Patricia, 46
Operation Wolf (video game), 30
outcasts, 44–45, 56
overreactions, 59–62

Paducah, Kentucky, school shootings in, 8, 20
Paducah Tilghman High School, 12–13
parents, 33, 34, 63–68, 89–90
Paxil, 48, 51, 54
Pearl, Mississippi, shootings in, 11
personalization technology, 68–71
play, effects of, 37–38
police, 27
prison study, 43–44
problems, social, 14–15, 18–20, 24, 27
profiling, 15

Prozac, 48
psychosis, 46, 48–49, 52
psychotropic drugs, 48

rampage shootings, 10–17, 46–47, 72–73
Red Lake High School, shootings at, 55–56, 58, 63–66, 68–69, 71–74
Reeve, Christopher, 83
regimentation, 77–78
revenge, 15, 45, 60
robberies, 21
Ruegsegger, Kacey, 83–85

Santana High School, shootings at, 12, 19
schools
    safety of, 14–15, 22, 59, 74–75, 76–77
    violence in, 10, 17–22, 27, 30, 32, 45, 60–61, 77–78
school shootings
    are a serious problem, 10–17
    con, 18–27, 75
    causes of, 28–62
    prevention of, 63–81
    victims of, 82–90
security measures, 15, 27, 60–61, 69, 75, 77
seizures, 46, 52
selective serotonin reuptake inhibitors (SSRIs), 46, 48–49, 51–54
self-defense, 66–67
September 11, 2001, attacks, 16, 27
Sims, The (video game), 35
single-victim homicides, 16
smart guns, 68–71
Smith & Wesson, 71
sniper video games, 7–9, 28
Solomon, T.J., 11

Solvay Pharmaceuticals, Inc., 47, 49, 50–54
Splinter Cell (video game), 30
sports, 57
    see also athletes
Springfield, Oregon, shootings in, 11, 20
Stamps, Arkansas, shootings in, 11
statistics, 8, 14–22, 24, 26–27, 30, 75, 77
stereotypes, sexist, 35
students, 13
suburbs, 12–13, 23, 76
suicides, 14, 21, 50–52, 55

Taylor, Mark, 46–47, 49–54
teachers, 63–67, 76–79
teenagers, violence and, 13, 17–19, 21–22, 32–34, 36, 44–45, 60–61
television, 7, 63, 65
terrorism, 61
    see also September 11, 2001, attacks
testing programs, 76–81
Thompson, Jack, 28
threats, 17, 60
Todd, Joseph, 11
Townsend, Lauren, 88
Townsend, Sue, 88
trench coats, 7, 44, 47, 56, 60

university campuses, shootings on, 16

urban areas, 12–13, 15, 17, 23
U.S.-Iraq War, 61

victimization, 22, 44, 56, 77
video games, 7–9
    regulation of, 7–9
    school shootings caused by, 28–31
        con, 32–38, 56–57, 63, 65
    see also specific video games
violence, 7–9, 12–13, 15–18, 23, 36, 43, 55–59
    see also schools, violence in

Wahluke High School, 54
weapons, 22, 58
    concealed, 63, 66–67
    see also assault weapons; guns
Weise, Jeff, 55–56, 68–69, 73–74
Wellsboro, Pennsylvania, shootings in, 29–30
Williams, Charles Andrew (Andy), 12
women, 34–35, 57
Woodham, Luke, 11
workplace homicides, 16
Wurst, Andrew, 11

youth. *See* teenagers, violence and
youth homicides, 17
Youth Risk Behavior Survey, 22

zero-tolerance policies, 15, 61
Zimbardo, Phillip, 43–44
Zoloft, 48